Child in the Manger

The True Meaning of Christmas

Sinclair B. Ferguson

Child in the manger,
Infant of Mary;
Outcast and stranger,
Lord of all!

THE BANNER OF TRUTH TRUST

THE BANNER OF TRUTH TRUST

3 Murrayfield Road, Edinburgh EH12 6EL, UK
PO Box 621, Carlisle, PA 17013, USA

© Sinclair B. Ferguson, 2015

ISBN

Print: 978 1 84871 655 1
EPUB: 978 1 84871 656 8
Kindle: 978 1 84871 657 5

Typeset in 11/14 pt Adobe Garamond Pro
at the Banner of Truth Trust, Edinburgh

Printed in the USA by
Versa Press, Inc.,
East Peoria, IL

To

The Members

of

The First Presbyterian Church
Columbia, South Carolina

With Gratitude and Affection

Contents

Introduction

The best-known phrase written by Charles Dickens, author of *A Christmas Carol*, is probably 'It was the best of times, it was the worst of times.'

But the words are not found in *A Christmas Carol*. Instead they are part of the opening sentence of *A Tale of Two Cities*. However, they well sum up reactions to Christmas. It means different things to different people.

On the one hand it often means holidays, parties, family gatherings, presents, meals together, music, and special events.

On the other hand for many it can mean unwanted pressure, an increased sense of loneliness, family squabbles, and crowded shops. Plus, if you live in many parts of the Northern Hemisphere it takes place at the onset of winter with its cold weather and short days. There are more incidents of depression at Christmas time than at any other time of the year. It is indeed the best of times for some, but the worst of times for others.

Christmas is also the most commercialised holiday of the year. Many companies depend on the Christmas market. Without it the incentive for people to purchase items they would never otherwise buy would be lost, profits would go down, employment would be jeopardised, and some companies would be in danger of closing. And in addition it gives us all – or at least the majority of us – something to look forward to every year, even if, as is true for example in the United Kingdom, it is just to have an extended break at the turn of the year.

But Christmas is also a very elusive thing, isn't it? We look forward to it. But what is 'it'? Every year our pop stars and media personalities are asked the same unimaginative question, 'What does Christmas mean to you?', and give the understandably predictable answers: 'It's a time for the children.' 'It's about peace.' 'It's about family.' 'It's about gifts, but it's a pity it has become so commercialised.'

There is no other annual event in which almost everyone participates in the same activities at the same time of year. Birthdays, anniversaries, births, deaths, marriages, holidays, other festivals – these are experienced only by individuals or by groups of families and friends. Christmas is different. It 'means' something to everyone – even agnostics, to their embarrassment, seem to feel obliged to acknowledge it. I have never forgotten overhearing one of my professors – a vice president of the British Humanist Association, no less – asking an assistant in the university bookshop: 'Do you stock Christmas cards?' Almost everybody celebrates it in one form or another.

But why? What is it really all about? Does it actually have any 'meaning'?

Child in the Manger – The True Meaning of Christmas
sets out to explore that question. When we find the answer
we realise that it isn't only for Christmas time. So these
pages are an invitation to explore what that meaning
is. And if this book has come into your hands around
Christmas time, I pray that it will help you to enjoy it in
a new way.

As always the completion of a book increases my
gratitude to and for my wife Dorothy and our family. I
am grateful to the staff at the Banner of Truth Trust for
their encouragement and enthusiasm for this project.
The dedication is a simple expression of appreciation
for a wonderful congregation who made room for us as
strangers, and welcomed us as part of their church family,
and among whom we have spent some of our happiest
days.

Sinclair B. Ferguson
August 2015

A Question, a Parable, and a Family Tree

Glasgow is the largest city (although not the capital) of Scotland.

As visitors from all over the world discovered during the Commonwealth Games in the summer of 2014, it is a remarkably friendly city, in many ways a large village. It is also very much a city whose fortunes were increased by the expansion of the British Empire in the eighteenth and nineteenth centuries. The evidence of this is even embedded in the names of its city centre streets (West Nile Street, Jamaica Street) and perhaps even more so in the magnificent George Square which overlooks the City Chambers, the centre of local government. The square itself is dominated by monuments, but may well be, as the best-selling travel writer Bill Bryson claimed, the 'handsomest in Britain'. I would like to think so, although we Glaswegians (as people from Glasgow are called) might query the choice of adjective.

But what has George Square to do with Christmas? That question is in some ways the origin of this book.

I was born and bred in Glasgow. There is an often-repeated and largely true saying that 'You can take the boy out of Glasgow, but you cannot take Glasgow out of the boy.' And so, while much of my life has been spent away from it, for a variety of reasons I have been in my home city for more than half of my Christmas Eves.

Over the years I developed a personal Christmas Eve ritual *en route* to the Christmas Eve church service. I parked my car in an unaccustomed spot to the east of the square and walked across it to the city centre church where as a teenager I had first become a Christian, and later at different periods of my life I had served as a minister.

The ritual began simply enough. One year I could not find a parking space near the church. Then I realised that the longer walk across the city square provided a few more minutes for quiet reflection *en route* to the Christmas Eve service. Time to drink in the atmosphere of Christmas Eve, and to watch the families who had come into town to see the giant Christmas tree and the Christmas lights.

As a Christian, and sometimes on my way to talk about the meaning of Christmas, this brief annual pilgrimage always put me in a pensive mood – one reason I retraced my steps from year to year.

I wondered about the parents there in the square with their children. Did they know what the lights and music were all originally intended to represent? Were these mums relieved to be out of the house for an hour or two, because Christmas was an annual strain on their physical and emotional resources? Did they find in the music and lights and surrounding laughter some respite from their anxieties about family and food and presents, and perhaps also finances?

I also wondered about the children. What were they expecting would happen in the next twelve hours or so? And would they discover in the next twenty-four hours that whatever 'happens' at Christmas does not last? And I also wondered: Do they know anything about the Christmas story?

This may seem a melancholy meditation for Christmas Eve! Yet it was not an accident that these thoughts passed through my mind. Every year there would be many people like those I watched in the square who would be at Christmas Eve services. What would they hear? Would they discover what Christmas was really all about?

Two particular images are etched in my mental memory bank from those years. One provokes a question; the other forms a parable.

A question

At some point over the years a large banner appeared on the south side of the square. It carried a message from the Lord Provost (the Scottish equivalent of the mayor in other cultures, traditionally named the 'Lord' Provost, although the role itself guaranteed no honour from the Queen, nor a seat in the House of Lords in the British Parliament!).

The wording on the banner conveyed the Lord Provost's greetings to the city:

May I take this opportunity to wish
Happy Christmas and a Peaceful and Prosperous New Year
to all citizens and visitors alike.
I hope and pray that the true meaning of Christmas
will be in everybody's minds and hearts
at this particular time of year.

It provoked in me, and I imagine in many others, the obvious question: What is the *true meaning* of Christmas'? How would we explain it to an alien visitor from outer space who happened to land in George Square on Christmas Eve? But much more pressing on my mind was always the question: 'These children and their parents who are enjoying this bright scene – what do they make of our Lord Provost's greeting? Will any of these mums and dads find a little face turned questioningly up at them and a little voice saying, "Mummy, Daddy, what *is* the true meaning of Christmas?"'

A parable

On the north side of the square stood a massive manger scene – a life-size representation of the stable, Mary and Joseph, the manger complete with baby, and various shepherds and wise men. One year as I made my way to church I noticed two police officers standing beside it as if on guard.

Glasgow is a friendly city, none friendlier. It is said that if a stranger asks a Glaswegian for directions, the latter will say, 'I was just going that way. Come with me' – despite the fact that the Glaswegian was, apparently, heading in the opposite direction! So it is usually quite safe to smile at or nod to a Glasgow police officer. But I have often wondered if it is ever appropriate to say something to them. But of all evenings Christmas Eve was surely one on which a friendly word, a greeting, even a passing question might result in a brief conversation.

And so I made a statement, inflecting it so that it sounded like a question. For all I knew they might have been going off duty just as our late night service was about to begin and decide to come along to hear what I had to say.

So I said, with a smile: 'Guarding the manger?'

I hoped it might open up an interesting conversation – after all, the whole point of the original manger was that in it lay the baby who had come to guard us. Did we not read each year in our Christmas services: 'To us a child is born, to us a son is given, and the government shall be upon his shoulder, and his name shall be called Wonderful Counsellor, Mighty God, Everlasting Father, Prince of Peace'?[1] There was something paradoxical about police officers guarding him!

The officers' answer took me by surprise: 'Well, yes. We are guarding the manger. You see last year the baby Jesus was stolen!'

So the previous year one might have stood in George Square with the Lord Provost's message on the south side with its hope that we might all know 'the true meaning of Christmas', while on the north side the 'baby' who represented the true meaning of Christmas had been stolen!

It struck me as a parable. We continue to wish for the blessings of Christmas; but we have lost the benefactor. The

[1] Isaiah 9:6.

central figure is no longer central in the whole business. For many people the baby has been stolen.

How can we find him and rediscover the *true* meaning of Christmas?

We need to go back to the beginning.

Back to the beginning

The New Testament was originally written in Greek. But even if you knew only the letters of the Greek alphabet you could translate its opening words:

Biblos geneseōs Iēsou Christou.

Think:

'Bible' (*Biblos* book);

'of the genesis' (*geneseōs* from *genesis* beginning);

'of Jesus Christ' (*Iēsou Christou*):

'The Book of the genesis of Jesus Christ.'

Matthew is the 'Genesis' of the New Testament!

Genesis, the first book in the Old Testament, opens with the actions of God that brought about the beginnings of the cosmos, the earth, and the creation of Adam. Similarly the first book of the New Testament begins with the actions of God that eventually brought about the birth of Jesus Christ.

Matthew was one of Jesus' earliest disciples.[1] Unlike the other three Gospel writers he begins his account of Jesus' life by setting it within the framework of many centuries

[1] Matthew 9:9.

of history. But he does so in the most abbreviated way possible: by means of a family tree – Jesus' genealogy. He traces the story behind his life back to Abraham.

In essence the message is: the significance of the birth of Jesus can be fully understood only when we see where it fits into the big picture.

Here is that big picture – it may seem tedious:

The book of the genealogy of Jesus Christ, the son of David, the son of Abraham. Abraham was the father of Isaac, and Isaac the father of Jacob, and Jacob the father of Judah and his brothers, and Judah the father of Perez and Zerah by Tamar, and Perez the father of Hezron, and Hezron the father of Ram, and Ram the father of Amminadab, and Amminadab the father of Nahshon, and Nahshon the father of Salmon, and Salmon the father of Boaz by Rahab, and Boaz the father of Obed by Ruth, and Obed the father of Jesse, and Jesse the father of David the king.

And David was the father of Solomon by the wife of Uriah, and Solomon the father of Rehoboam, and Rehoboam the father of Abijah, and Abijah the father of Asaph, and Asaph the father of Jehoshaphat, and Jehoshaphat the father of Joram, and Joram the father of Uzziah, and Uzziah the father of Jotham, and Jotham the father of Ahaz, and Ahaz the father of Hezekiah, and Hezekiah the father of Manasseh, and Manasseh the father of Amos, and Amos the father of Josiah, and Josiah the father of Jechoniah and his brothers, at the time of the deportation to Babylon.

And after the deportation to Babylon: Jechoniah was the father of Shealtiel, and Shealtiel the father of Zerubbabel, and Zerubbabel the father of Abiud, and Abiud the father of Eliakim, and Eliakim the father of Azor, and Azor the father of Zadok, and Zadok the father of Achim, and Achim the father of Eliud, and Eliud the father of Eleazar, and Eleazar the father of Matthan, and Matthan the father of Jacob, and Jacob the father of Joseph the husband of Mary, of whom Jesus was born, who is called Christ.

So all the generations from Abraham to David were fourteen generations, and from David to the deportation to Babylon fourteen generations, and from the deportation to Babylon to the Christ fourteen generations.[1]

Boring?

Even an enthusiastic reader occasionally groans when a biography begins with an extended description of the subject's family tree. If it took the author months to research it to the last detail, why does he or she think a reader can absorb it all in a few minutes? Better simply to put the genealogy in a visual chart somewhere, and then tell us the few details we need to know. We can learn more later on when our interest has been aroused.

This is probably the reason Matthew 1:1-17 is rarely read in Christmas services. It is not just that the names are unfamiliar and therefore difficult to read with confidence; it simply sounds so boring to most of us. It does nothing to encourage the 'feel good' factor expected in a Christmas service. Many people will say, 'I love the Sermon on the Mount'[2] (even if they have never read the whole of it),

[1] Matthew 1:1-17.
[2] Matthew 5:1 – 7:29.

but has anyone ever said, 'I really love the introduction to Matthew's Gospel'?

So why did Matthew make this elementary mistake in the opening section of his Gospel?

It wasn't a mistake. He was saying: 'You will not fully understand what I am about to tell you in this book unless you read it in the context of the big picture represented by this family tree.'

So here is a family tree. Right at the very end of it Matthew writes:

> So all the generations from Abraham to David were fourteen generations, and from David to the deportation to Babylon[1] fourteen generations, and from the deportation to Babylon to the Christ fourteen generations.[2]

Three groups of fourteen generations is unusually tidy! In fact the neatness is a signal to us that this is not a complete genealogy. Matthew has deliberately missed out various generations in his storyline. It was never his intention to give an exhaustive family tree. Instead his big message is 'I want you to understand that there is a pattern here.'

But what is the pattern?

And why does it begin with Abraham?

[1] The 'deportation to Babylon' is a reference to the Babylonian exile which followed the fall of Jerusalem to King Nebuchadnezzar (16 March 597 B.C.). This cataclysmic event during the reign of King Jehoiachin is described in 2 Kings 24:8 – 29:30 and Daniel 1:1-4.

[2] Matthew 1:17.

Beginning with Abraham

Matthew had the same Hebrew Bible we have.[1] He knew that Abraham's father was called Terah, and that his family tree was embedded in the early chapters of Genesis. So why not go further back? After all, Luke did in his genealogy.[2] There surely must be a reason for the difference?

Now the genealogy is a little more intriguing. In fact it contains a kind of code. We are being invited to work it out for ourselves. Why would Matthew – himself a Jew, a son of Abraham, of the tribe of Levi[3] – do this? The message is this: to understand this Gospel we need to go back to the Old Testament story of Abraham.

God promised Abraham that he would bring blessing to all the nations of the world through his family line:

> I will make you into a great nation
>   and I will bless you;
> I will make your name great,
>   and you will be a blessing.
> I will bless those who bless you,
>   and whoever curses you I will curse;
> *and all peoples on earth will be blessed through you.*[4]

Now what follows makes more sense.

---

[1] That is, what Christians call the Old Testament. The books were, however, listed in a different order.

[2] See Luke 3:23-38. Luke traces Jesus' genealogy all the way back to Adam, because he is working with a different but complementary 'big picture': Adam was the 'first man'; Jesus has come as the 'second man' and the 'last Adam' (1 Corinthians 15:45).

[3] Mark 2:14; Luke 5:27.

[4] Genesis 12:2-3 NIV.

Matthew's Gospel –

• Begins with the promise of God to bless the nations and

• Ends with the apostles being told to go to all the nations (or peoples) with the good news of the gospel.[1]

Thus the beginning of the Gospel reminds us of the promise of blessing for the nations; the end of the Gospel tells us that this promise would be fulfilled through the coming of Christ, the mission of his apostles, and his presence with the church to the end of the age. So the way in which the Abrahamic promise is fulfilled in Christ and will be consummated through Christ is the big picture that makes sense of everything else.[2]

From David onwards

Fast-forward through the first section of the genealogy and we come to David.

God promised David that his throne would last forever.[3]

From time to time, the Psalms reflect on this kingdom

---

[1] Matthew 28:18-20.

[2] There are, of course, other layers of significance in the genealogy. Thus, for example, biblical genealogies are male-dominated, as indeed this one also is. But there are five notable exceptions. Tamar, Rahab, Ruth, and Bathsheba are mentioned. Tamar is in the family tree only because she conceived her twins by deceiving her father-in-law; Rahab was a Canaanite prostitute; Ruth was a Moabitess; Bathsheba committed adultery with David and thus precipitated her husband's planned death. Then, of course, there is Mary. In this sense Jesus' genealogy signals that he has really entered into our fallen world, and that he came for sinners, and indeed for Gentiles too, like Rahab and Ruth.

[3] 2 Samuel 7:16.

and look forward to the day when a great king would rule far beyond the borders of David's kingdom.[1] It is this kingdom – the kingdom of God – that Matthew is about to tell us has been inaugurated in Jesus' coming.

Matthew then extends his narrative to 'the deportation to Babylon' – the exile when many of God's people were forcibly taken from Jerusalem and from the land God had promised would be theirs so long as they remained faithful to him. They had sinned and rebelled against him. Tragically they assumed God did not really mean it when he said that sin would lead to their exile. But his promises – including his promises of judgment – came true. The people became captives in Babylon. Had God's promise failed? No. This was exactly what he had said would happen if they sinned.[2]

But that was not the end of his promise. The people's rebellion against God's covenant made with Moses could not destroy the prior covenant made with Abraham! So now Matthew shows how God was faithful to his promise to Abraham. He preserved the royal line. But it was greatly reduced in honour. He traces it to a lowly carpenter and a young woman from Nazareth. But into their lives God now entrusts 'the Christ', the promised seed of Abraham.[3]

This genealogy is an amazing story of God's faithfulness to his promise to bless all the nations of the earth.

---

[1] For example, Psalm 2:8; Psalm 72:1-11.
[2] See Deuteronomy 28:58-63.
[3] Matthew 1:17.

What happened next?

This international element in the promise to Abraham helps us to understand the significance of the events Matthew now records:

> Now after Jesus was born in Bethlehem of Judea in the days of Herod the king, wise men from the east came to Jerusalem, saying, 'Where is he who has been born king of the Jews? For we saw his star when it rose and have come to worship him.'[1]

Now it becomes clear what is happening. The blessing of the nations is already beginning. The coming of visitors from among the *goyim*, the nations, serves as a sign that God is keeping his ancient promise. It is beginning to be fulfilled in Jesus – even in his infancy.

So, Matthew is telling us that the direction, the goal, and the meaning of this history are all found in the baby who was born in Bethlehem.

This is what Phillips Brooks (1835–93), Episcopalian Bishop of Massachusetts, expressed so beautifully in his much-loved Christmas hymn:

> O little town of Bethlehem,
>   How still we see thee lie!
> Above thy deep and dreamless sleep
>   The silent stars go by:
> Yet in thy dark streets shineth
>   The everlasting Light;
> *The hopes and fears of all the years*
>   *Are met in thee tonight.*

[1] Matthew 2:1-2.

That sums up Matthew's message: 'The hopes and fears of all the years are met in thee tonight.'

The birth of Jesus divided history into two major epochs. Until the dawn of our hyper-sensitive age, even the way we dated events underscored this. From time immemorial every day, every week, every month, every year has been described as either 'B.C.' ('Before Christ') or 'A.D.' (*Anno Domini*, 'in the year of our Lord'). Even the modern, pluralistic style abbreviations, B.C.E. ('Before the Common Era') and C.E. ('Common Era'), cannot obliterate the indelible impress of Jesus' birth. For what makes the 'Common Era' so 'common'? And what explains the dividing line date? The answer is the same: the birth of Jesus. At the very centre of history stands the person of Jesus Christ. And he does so because he is at the centre of God's story.

Joseph

It comes as something of a surprise however that in Matthew's account of the incarnation it is Joseph, not Mary, who takes centre-stage:

> Now the birth of Jesus Christ took place in this way. When his mother Mary had been betrothed to Joseph, before they came together she was found to be with child from the Holy Spirit. And her husband Joseph, being a just man and unwilling to put her to shame, resolved to divorce her quietly. But as he considered these things, behold, an angel of the Lord appeared to him in a dream, saying, 'Joseph, son of David, do not fear to take Mary as your wife, for that which is conceived in her is from the Holy Spirit. She will bear a son, and you shall call his

name Jesus, for he will save his people from their sins.'
All this took place to fulfil what the Lord had spoken by
the prophet:

> 'Behold, the virgin shall conceive and bear a son,
>   and they shall call his name Immanuel' (which
>   means, God with us).

When Joseph woke from sleep, he did as the angel of
the Lord commanded him: he took his wife, but knew
her not until she had given birth to a son. And he called
his name Jesus.[1]

Joseph is described as a 'just' (*dikaios*) man. This carries
much more significance than our modern idea of being
just. *Dikaios* means being 'righteous' – a person who has
a faithful covenant relationship with God because of his
grace. To be 'righteous' does not mean being innocent or
sin-free. It means trusting in God's provision for forgiveness and new life and living in fellowship with him. Luke
describes several other people in the same way.[2]

So someone (like Joseph) described as *dikaios* trusted
in God's covenant grace, believed his promises, and lived
in the knowledge of his forgiveness and love. Life thus had
meaning: to know and love the Lord and to love and serve
others. The 'righteous' were, simply put, the real believers.

To put it in the much later famous words of *The Westminster Shorter Catechism*, they were people whose lives
had been so touched by God's love that they wanted to
'glorify God and enjoy him for ever'.

[1] Matthew 1:18-25.
[2] John the Baptist's parents, Zechariah and Elizabeth, as well as the
aged Simeon whom Mary and Joseph later meet in the temple at Jerusalem (Luke 1:6; 2:25).

But in a moment Joseph's life was dramatically changed. Mary was pregnant. His world was shattered.

Hopes dashed

The only thing Joseph could be sure about was that he was not the father. The unthinkable had happened. His world must have swung off its hinges. Mary was expecting a child. There was only one conclusion he could draw.

What is Joseph to do? He cannot go on with the marriage; he is a righteous man. But he is betrothed and that was a legally binding contract. He must seek to dissolve it. But it is a *public* contract – everyone will know. The situation is his worst nightmare. His soul aches with multi-layered disappointments. But Joseph is a righteous man because he has experienced God's grace. And so he in turn seeks to do the gracious thing: to divorce Mary quietly, with the least degree of embarrassment possible – for Mary's sake, for the sake of both his and her parents, and for his own sake. But how could he possibly do that? This was rural first-century Ancient Near East. How could this be hidden? Mary is ruined. Life has come to a grinding halt, and Joseph is staring into a black hole.

Joseph does not yet know that it is God's action that has momentarily shattered his life. God sometimes does that. But only because he knows exactly what he plans to accomplish.

I still wonder what happened to a man who came to see me at the close of a daily service in the city centre church where I was a young staff minister. I was twenty-three years old and had lived a relatively sheltered life. The man was perhaps fifteen to twenty years older than I was. I soon realised that he could have bought and sold me many times over. But no amount of material success compensated or comforted him now. He had been wandering the streets of Glasgow, distraught almost beyond words. Life had been turned on its head. His wife had just been told she was terminally ill. Everything now lay in ruins. He had nowhere to go, and no one to whom he could turn. We spoke together that morning, and I tried to point him to the only One who is able to help. But we never met again. Did he ever find the comfort and grace of Jesus Christ? If he is still alive he does not know how often I have thought of him.

Joseph was facing a similar crisis, but with a twist. He would feel the wound every time someone who knew his story entered his workshop. He would wonder if every new customer was secretly wondering whether he could be trusted. What he did not yet know – until God sent a message that simultaneously comforted him, stretched his faith, and challenged him – was this: the shattering of his hopes and expectations was the prelude to the discovery of the central purpose of his whole life.

From now on everything would revolve around Jesus.

Joseph was of course a specific individual in history. But his experience is also a dramatic illustration of how God works. Whenever Christ enters a life everything is rearranged around him as its new centre.

The final movement

The enigmatic book of Ecclesiastes tells us that God has

> made everything beautiful in its time. Also, he has put
> eternity into man's heart, yet so that he cannot find out
> what God has done from the beginning to the end.[1]

In a word, we are surrounded by testimonies to God's goodness and beauty. We are also invaded by a sense that we were made for eternity. We can never, therefore, be satisfied with this world in and of itself. If we were created for the eternal, nothing less than the Eternal One can satisfy us.

Did Joseph think that Mary would provide the satisfaction he needed? He would have been disappointed. She was never intended to bring ultimate meaning to his life. Now they were both being led to a better and more satisfying fountain, Jesus, the Saviour.

C. S. Lewis, the distinguished English literature scholar, had a novel way of illustrating how the Bible story works, which can be developed as follows.

Imagine that a famous composer had written a great symphony, so marvellous that it was played all over the world. Yet whenever it was played, orchestras and their conductors, musicologists, critics, and audiences all felt exactly the same thing: the music left its hearers with a sense of being incomplete, unfinished, as though there was 'something else to come'.

Then a researcher discovers a hitherto uncatalogued manuscript in the composer's handwriting. It is an

[1] Ecclesiastes 3:11.

astonishing piece of music in its own right. In some respects it is mysterious, difficult fully to understand, and yet magnificent. There are elements in it that are wholly unexpected. Then the truth begins to dawn: *this is the missing final movement.* When played as the climax of the symphony it does two things. First, it makes sense of the whole, and removes its incompleteness. Then, second, it not only makes sense of the earlier movements but seems to take over the whole, as if the first three movements, for all their greatness, were but a stepping-stone or a series of clues to the final movement.

Matthew's Gospel works just like that. It opens with a summary of the three movements of the Old Testament: Abraham to David; David to the Exile; the Exile to the Birth. Marvellous, yet enigmatic and incomplete. But now begins the final movement and the entire symphony makes sense.

As is well known, C. S. Lewis himself knew a great deal about incompleteness in his own life.[1] As a young man he fashionably became an intellectual agnostic. But then he began to hear a new kind of music. Its strains slowly came over him through the authors he read and then through the lives of friends. Usually when that begins to happen, the music gets louder, clearer, more attractive – at times almost unbearably so – because it highlights our lack of beauty, our life in sin. But then the music leads us to the Musician, and we discover that he is also the Composer and Conductor. He has written the score, conducted the

[1] He tells the story in his autobiographical *Surprised by Joy* (London: Fontana, 1955).

symphony, and led the orchestra himself. And we are caught up in the wonder of it all. We heard the music, now we see the one who composed it and makes sense of it.

This is what happens when we discover 'the *true* meaning of Christmas'. This is how the Bible story plays out. It makes sense of the world's story – and also, marvellously, of our lives within it. The music invades us, and we yield to it. And our hearts respond in trust and wonder and praise.

The dawning of the light

There is a statement in the Psalms that sums this up perfectly: 'In your light we see light.'[1] Matthew is teaching us that when we see the significance of the coming of the Lord Jesus Christ – 'he will save his people from their sins' – it is as if someone has switched on a light in our minds.

Of course we do not understand everything; the gospel does not turn us into leading intellectuals! But we do come to understand *something* about everything, namely that in Christ everything begins to make sense.

This is why John wrote in the Prologue to his Gospel that in Jesus light came into the world.[2] Later he recorded Jesus' own words:

> I am the light of the world.
> Whoever follows me will not walk in darkness,
>   but will have the light of life.[3]

This, then, is the meaning of Christmas: the Light of the world has come into the darkness of the world, in order

[1] Psalm 36:9 NIV.
[2] John 1:4-9.
[3] John 8:12.

to bring light into the darkness of our hearts, and to illumine them with the grace of forgiveness.

When we see this, we not only sing about 'the hopes and fears of all the years' being met in Christ; we also pray to him in words such as these from the same hymn:

> How silently, how silently,
>   The wondrous Gift is giv'n!
> So God imparts to human hearts
>   The blessings of His heaven.
> No ear may hear His coming;
>   But in this world of sin,
> Where meek souls will receive Him, still
>   The dear Christ enters in.
>
> O holy Child of Bethlehem,
>   Descend to us, we pray;
> Cast out our sin, and enter in;
>   Be born in us today.
> We hear the Christmas angels
>   The great glad tidings tell;
> O come to us, abide with us,
>   Our Lord Emmanuel.

Of course there is more to the gospel than this; much more. But there is never less. It is possible for us to be born again, born from above, and for our lives to begin anew in Christ![1]

So, basic to 'the true meaning of Christmas' is this: God has kept his promises. The seed of Abraham, the Son of David, has come into the world to bring the blessing of salvation to believers in every nation. Christ who – as we

---

[1] See John 3:1-14.

shall see in the next chapter – is the Creator of all things, has entered his own creation in order to become our Saviour. That is what gives Christmas meaning. It is what gives history meaning. And it gives our lives meaning too.

Joseph must have often looked at Jesus and thought: 'So you are the one who was promised. You are *Jesus*. You are the one who has come to save your people from their sins. Now I know that this includes me.'

Does it include you? Have you ever said to Jesus what Joseph said?[1]

So Joseph discovered the true meaning of Christmas. But this meaning goes back further yet, as we will see in the next chapter.

[1] Joseph does not personally appear in the narrative of the Gospels after Jesus is twelve years old (Luke 2:41-52). It is generally assumed that he died before Jesus began his public ministry at the age of thirty. So he did not live to see exactly how Jesus would fulfil the promise of God. In that sense he was one of the last of a long line of Old Testament believers who trusted God's promise but did not live to see its fulfilment. Joseph however knew more than any of them – he knew the promised Messiah was Jesus. At the same time Joseph's faith illustrates an important principle. We may not be able fully to explain how it is that Jesus saves us by his death and resurrection. But if we know enough about him to trust that he does, then like Joseph we too can call him 'Jesus, Saviour from sin'.

2

Word Made Flesh

The big word used to describe what Christians all over the world celebrate at Christmas time is 'Incarnation'. Like many English words it is derived from Latin: the preposition *in* meaning the same in English, and the word for flesh (*carnis*). The staggering claim of the Christian gospel is that God the Son took human flesh.

The opening chapter of John's Gospel describes this miracle in simple words:

> And the Word became flesh and dwelt among us.[1]

This is the heart of the matter. It is difficult to imagine a more profound statement in any literature in any language. The climax to the Prologue to John's Gospel describes the unfathomable.

Here is the whole Prologue:

> In the beginning was the Word, and the Word was with God, and the Word was God. He was in the beginning

---

[1] John 1:14. The same emphasis is found in Luke 1:31-32, 35.

with God. All things were made through him, and without him was not any thing made that was made. In him was life, and the life was the light of men. The light shines in the darkness, and the darkness has not overcome it.

There was a man sent from God, whose name was John. He came as a witness, to bear witness about the light, that all might believe through him. He was not the light, but came to bear witness about the light.

The true light, which gives light to everyone, was coming into the world. He was in the world, and the world was made through him, yet the world did not know him. He came to his own, and his own people did not receive him. But to all who did receive him, who believed in his name, he gave the right to become children of God, who were born, not of blood nor of the will of the flesh nor of the will of man, but of God.

And the Word became flesh and dwelt among us, and we have seen his glory, glory as of the only Son from the Father, full of grace and truth. (John bore witness about him, and cried out, 'This was he of whom I said, "He who comes after me ranks before me, because he was before me."') For from his fullness we have all received, grace upon grace. For the law was given through Moses; grace and truth came through Jesus Christ. No one has ever seen God; the only God, who is at the Father's side, he has made him known.

What does all this mean?

The Word of God

It is a strange thing to describe a person as a 'word'. But John makes clear what he means: the person we know as Jesus of Nazareth existed before he was born.

He expresses this in a series of majestic statements:

In the beginning was the Word,
   and the Word was with God,
   and the Word was God.
He was in the beginning with God.
All things were made through him,
   and without him was not any thing made
   that was made.[1]

To begin with, John is obviously and deliberately echoing the opening words of the Bible. In fact his first words *are* the first words in the Bible: 'In the beginning …'

The first readers of this Gospel were almost certainly very familiar with Genesis chapter 1.[2] Given our tendency to word association, whenever they heard 'In the beginning', the next word in their minds would have been 'God'.[3] But in fact John takes us by surprise. He writes: 'In the beginning … *was the Word.*' – 'In that same beginning', he is saying, 'was the Word, and the Word was with God, and was God.'

John is transporting us back through time and bringing us to a point *before* creation, *before* time (if we can use such language). He brings us to a 'time before time' and makes a staggering claim about Jesus – whom he had known so well: He was there as the Word in the beginning. He was the Word through which God spoke the cosmos

---

[1] John 1:1-3.

[2] There are so many allusions to the Old Testament in John's Gospel that it seems certain he expected his readers to be familiar with it.

[3] If anything this tendency to word association would have been even stronger in readers and listeners familiar with the Hebrew Bible which abounds in word associations.

into being. When Genesis recorded, 'And God said … and it was so', it meant that this Word acted.

Words have power. They communicate, but they also do something. My mother taught me as a child that

> Sticks and stones may break my bones,
> But words will never hurt me.

It did not take me long to discover that it was not true. Words can hurt. They have power. So does *the Word*.

But now we are taken one stage further –

The Word was with *God*

John's words[1] are traditionally rendered 'The Word was *with* God.' But they could just as easily be translated, 'The Word was *towards* God', or perhaps even paraphrased as 'The Word was *face to face* with God.'[2]

Different cultures have different etiquettes. In Western culture there is a widely recognised etiquette that governs the contact between a man and a woman: 'locking eyes' expresses a desire for intimacy. Say you are a young man and have a girlfriend. You notice her locking eyes with one of your friends. What do you feel? Betrayed by both. The

---

[1] *Ho Logos ēn pros ton Theon.*

[2] William Hendriksen, *A Commentary on the Gospel of John* (London: Banner of Truth Trust, 1959), 70: 'The New Testament contains more than 600 examples of πρός with the accusative. It indicates motion or direction toward a place, or as here, close proximity; hence friendship, intimacy, in this context.' H. N. Ridderbos comments similarly: 'Apparently "with God" (πρός + accusative) is intended as an indication not only of place but also of disposition and orientation.' *The Gospel of John, A Theological Commentary*, trans., John Vriend (Grand Rapids: Eerdmans, 1997), 25, fn. 23.

relationship you thought was developing has been invaded from the outside and set aside on the inside. Or you are a married man and you discover another man locking eyes with your wife. A kind of theft has taken place, which is the adultery of the eyes, about which Jesus spoke so severely.[1]

Intimacy

We all understand this etiquette of intimacy. But think of it as a window into the etiquette of heaven. Neither man nor angel may look on God and live, far less 'lock eyes' with him in the deepest intimacy of mutual devotion.[2] Yet John says that the Word of God could 'lock eyes' with God, drinking in his love, and returning it.

Later in his Prologue John tells us that the Word, the Son of God, was 'at the Father's side' or more literally 'in the bosom of the Father'.[3]

The second half of John's Gospel opens with Jesus and his disciples celebrating a Passover meal in a house in Jerusalem.[4] There Jesus washed his disciples' feet, including, apparently, those of Judas Iscariot.[5] Then he told them that one of them would betray him. Simon Peter indicated to John that he should ask the Master who it would be – something he was able to do because he was 'reclining at

[1] Matthew 5:27-30.

[2] Exodus 33:20. Think here of how the seraphim, who have never sinned and are perfectly holy, are nevertheless said to cover their faces before the face of the thrice-holy God (Isaiah 6:2).

[3] John 1:18.

[4] John 13:1-20.

[5] Judas does not leave the room until afterwards (John 13:30).

table close to Jesus'.[1] Here John repeats the same language he had used to describe the relationship of the Word to God. John was reclining 'in the bosom of Jesus' – just as the Word was 'in the bosom of the Father'.[2]

John uses this expression on only these two occasions, perhaps in order to create an association of ideas: the deep friendship between John and Jesus is a reflection of the intimacy Jesus himself has with the Father. Did John look into Jesus' eyes as he asked his question: 'Lord, who is it?' And did he see there a reflection of Jesus himself 'in the bosom of the Father'?[3]

These statements John makes about Jesus are extraordinary. But there is more:

The Word was *God*

Jesus, the Word, displayed both the attributes and the unique activities of God. He has 'life in himself'.[4] 'All things were made through him, and without him was not any thing made that was made.'[5]

We might expect someone to say in response: 'Well, of course, that was just one person's opinion.'

Indeed it was one person's opinion: Jesus' opinion. Throughout the Gospel, he claims to be one with the Father, to be equal with the Father, to do the things the Father does, to speak with the authority of the Father, and to have shared the Father's glory.[6]

---

[1] John 13:23.
[2] See the marinal notes at John 1:18 and John 13:23 in the ESV.
[3] He seems to hint as much in John 13:3.
[4] John 5:26; 11:25. Cf. John 1:4.
[5] John 1:3.
[6] John 5:19-25; 8:58-59; 10:30-33; 17:5.

This, of course, is what sets Jesus apart from all other religious leaders. As C. S. Lewis wrote in a relatively obscure essay entitled 'What are we to make of Jesus Christ?' there is no parallel to this in other world religions:

> If you had gone to Buddha and asked him 'Are you the Son of Brahma?' he would have said 'My son, you are still in the vale of illusion.' If you had gone to Socrates and asked 'Are you Zeus?' he would have laughed at you. If you had gone to Mohammed and asked 'Are you Allah?' he would first have rent his clothes, and then cut your head off. And, if you had asked Confucius, 'Are you heaven?', I think he would probably have replied, 'Remarks which are not in accordance with nature are in bad taste.'[1]

Lewis's point – which is by no means original to him – is that it makes no sense to accept Jesus as 'a great moral teacher, but not as God' in the way many people rather unthinkingly do ('I don't believe all the stuff about Jesus being Saviour and God, but I do think he was a great moral teacher and a wonderful example'). If he were not who and what he claimed to be, he was very far from being a great moral teacher. He was either a deceiver or he was deceived. We ought not to ignore the fact that he was executed for blasphemy. While our society would not have executed him for that, nor would we honour him as a great teacher if he were either a liar or profoundly and sadly deceived.

We simply cannot wriggle round John's statement that Jesus is the Word who 'was with God, and was God'. If the

[1] C. S. Lewis, *God in the Dock* (Grand Rapids: Eerdmans, 1970), 157-58.

Gospel records are reliable witnesses to Jesus, we are forced into one of only three possibilities:

(1) He was what he claimed to be, or

(2) He was a liar, or

(3) He was seriously deluded and not fully responsible for what he said.

Yet the fact of the matter is *Jesus was a great moral teacher*. That fact increases the pressure on us to take seriously the claims made by him and for him.

What is all the more impressive is that the John who makes these points was one of a handful of human beings who knew the Word intimately. His testimony is: 'If you want to know who he really is, you must think of him in relation to eternity: he was in the beginning with God; indeed he was God.'[1]

But John would never have written his Gospel if that was all that was true. His story depends on the eternal Word also being related to time.

The Word became *flesh*

In relationship to eternity, Jesus is the Word of God; he is deity.

In relationship to time, however, we come to know him through his nativity: 'the Word became flesh'.

It is worth noticing that John does not say: 'God became man.' He is more precise than that. The Son of God did not change into something different, and cease to

---

[1] John's words are more fully explained in Sinclair B. Ferguson and Derek W. H. Thomas, *Ichthus* (Edinburgh: Banner of Truth, 2015), 6-9.

be God. Rather 'the Word [who was with God, and was God] became flesh'. He came to live in his own creation, as a member of our human race. Yet he never ceased to be the person he always was.

But why does he say 'The Word became *flesh*'?

The Greek word for flesh (*sarx*) has a range of meaning. It means flesh in the ordinary sense of 'flesh and blood', the soft tissue that covers our anatomy. But in John's day *sarx* also carried another layer of significance.

Every culture is heavily influenced by the perspectives embedded in its basic belief system. For example, in the twenty-first-century Western world we are heavily influenced by the philosophy of evolution. What started out as a way of explaining the development of organic life has mutated and has become a concept used in virtually every discipline. Thus people speak about our society 'evolving' morally. This, it is said, is why the moral norms, say of those who wrote the Constitution of the United States of America, are no longer normative today – society has evolved since then. Thus what starts out as a perspective held by a few can, over time, become part and parcel of the way a whole society thinks, a kind of cultural gene.

It is not long then until we assume that we see things as they really are, not realising that we view reality through mental lenses crafted by hidden presuppositions and personal commitments.

In antiquity world-views were influenced and shaped by the presupposition that there was a deep antithesis between spirit and matter or flesh. Reality was believed to have evolved (or more accurately de-volved) from the purely spiritual to the material. Anything material was therefore, by definition, less pure than the spiritual. Thus the material body, the flesh, was inevitably corrupted, unstable, and impure. The spiritual part of man, the soul, needed to escape from it. Thus the Greeks had a saying '*sōma sēma*' – 'the body is a tomb'. If there was such a thing as 'salvation' it was salvation *from* the body, not the salvation *of* the body.

This is why Paul was derided in Athens when he spoke about the resurrection of Jesus.[1] It was not merely that the Athenians thought the resurrection of a dead person was impossible. No, for them the idea that God would raise a dead body to life again was ludicrous. Why would he want to do that? Bodies are matter, flesh, by definition impure; we need to escape from them, not resurrect them!

So, in the context of the first century, John is making a very bold claim by saying 'the Word became flesh'. Not only did the Word who was with God and was God *not* despise material reality, he became part of it. Salvation comes not by us being delivered from the body but through the Word becoming flesh and taking a body!

Yet the Word of God remained everything he always was. But now he was all that in our human flesh – in all its weakness and frailty, dependent on God for everything, and constantly exposed to the assaults on his senses made by the fallen world.

Although he does not retell the story of Jesus' birth, John implies here that the Word became flesh in the form of an embryo. He lived within the dark chamber of his mother's womb in the fetal position. He became a tiny

[1] Acts 17:32.

human life, dependent on the nourishment he received from Mary – a small human speck in his own vast cosmos.

A few chapters later, John will tell us how Jesus became tired and thirsty.[1] And then a few chapters further on again, he will tell us how he was deeply moved by the death of a friend, how he wept, and how much he hated death because of the grief it brought to a family he loved.[2] Later, as the shadow of the cross grew longer and darker, his disciples sensed that he was deeply troubled. He said as much to them himself.[3] He did not seem to face his death as calmly as many Christians have faced theirs. Nor, for that matter, as readily as Socrates drank the hemlock in late fourth-century Athens for 'refusing to recognise the gods recognised by the state'.

Why did John and the other Gospel writers not hide or at least disguise and play down this sense of dread that Jesus experienced? Why display it in such detail? Because they understood that there was something unique about this death. It was a singularity: a death died under the unmitigated judgment of God against sin.

'The Word became flesh.' Yes, but then John adds that he 'dwelt among us'.

The Word dwelt *among us*

John's Gospel was written for people who were familiar with the Old Testament. When he wrote that 'the Word dwelt among us', he used a verb that would probably have

[1] John 4:6-7.
[2] John 11:33-35.
[3] Mark 14:33-34; John 13:21.

reminded them of the tabernacle or 'tent of meeting' in which Moses met with God during the wilderness wanderings following the exodus from Egypt.[1] It was the place where God came to 'dwell' among his people. And when Moses met with God there, his face shone with the reflection of the glory of God. He had to put a veil over his face to hide it.[2]

This reflected glory may seem strange to us. Yet we get glimpses of what it might mean. We meet friends who have had an enormous burden lifted from their lives – it is reflected on their faces. We meet a girl who has just got engaged – she knows now that she is loved in a unique way – it shows on her face; there is a kind of physical glow of joy, of release, of happiness, of contentment, of discovery of a hitherto unrealised destiny.

If this is true in ordinary life, what must it have been like for Moses when God met with him 'face to face, as a man speaks to his friend'?[3] No wonder his face shone!

But now, John is saying, when the Word became flesh, things were happening the other way round. Sinful Moses went inside the earthly tent to meet the glory of the God of heaven, and came out with his face reflecting that glory. But now the glory of the God of heaven has come into our 'earthly tent'[4] to meet sinful man! The Son, the Word – who is eternally with the Father, face to face with him,

---

[1] Exodus 25:8.

[2] Exodus 33:7-11; 34:34-35.

[3] Exodus 33:11.

[4] Paul uses this language to refer to the human body in 2 Corinthians 5:1-4.

gazing upon and enjoying the glory that emanates from him – has now become flesh in our fallen world. Now John and his friends have come to see the glory of God manifested in this one, unique person, Jesus.

What kind of glory is John talking about here?

Glory of the cross

At a critical point in Jesus' ministry he took Peter, James, and John up a mountain. There they saw him momentarily transformed. But, perhaps surprisingly, while the other three Gospels describe this event in some detail, John never mentions the transfiguration, even though he was one of the three disciples who witnessed it.[1] Instead what we find in John's Gospel is that the glory of Christ is related much more to his passion. Jesus is glorified in and through his death and resurrection.[2]

For John what reveals Christ's glory most clearly is the contrast between his eternal identity and his earthly experience. His native land was eternal glory. There he was worshipped and adored by seraphim and cherubim. He came from that world into the darkness of the virgin's womb. From there he emerged into the sinfulness of our broken and needy world. Eventually he turned a Roman gibbet into an altar, and in the darkness of Calvary offered himself to his Father as a sacrifice for our sins. That the Word who was with God should do this for us – this is his glory.

---

[1] All the other Gospels record the incident: Matthew 17:1-13; Mark 9:2-13; Luke 9:28-36.

[2] See John 7:39; 11:4; 12:23; 13:31-32; 17:1, 5, 24.

So, right at the very beginning of his Gospel John is saying: 'Let me first tell you what I will talk about in my Gospel: "The Eternal Word of God, through whom the whole cosmos was brought into being, has entered his world, become flesh and has dwelt among us. He has died on the cross for us and has been raised up again for us. In this 'we beheld his glory'."'

Think of it this way. You switch on the television in the middle of a documentary. The camera is fixed on a woman who is being interviewed – she fills the screen. All you see and know about her is that she has an amazing natural beauty; she also seems to have a wonderful poise and dignity. You are struck by her humble but striking intelligence, and by the graciousness of her character. Here is a woman who needs no make-up to improve her looks, no airbrushing to touch-up her photograph.

But then the camera angle widens. At first you had no context in which to interpret what you were seeing and hearing. But now you take in the background. Now you can see the context in which her beauty shines. She has not just come off the 'catwalk' at a fashion show. She is in the slums of India, surrounded by the Dalit – the traditional untouchables of the caste system. She is serving the poor, the hopeless, the diseased, the broken, and the marginalised. This woman loves the despised and the helpless and is giving her life to serve them.

Is she less glorious or more glorious for that? For this is where her glory is seen – in her willingness to give herself in all her beauty and graciousness for those who have none. Her presence shines in the darkness, and her dignity glows in the ugliness around her and brings hope and joy.

And then, as the programme ends and the credits roll across your television screen, you hear a voice saying, in broken English: 'I am a Dalit, yet she loved me; yes, she loved me as a Dalit!'

You could easily have one of two different reactions to this. You could be in awe of this woman. Or you could say 'What a waste!'

Something similar to this – only on a much grander scale – took place when 'The Word became flesh and dwelt among us, and we have seen his glory.'[1]

> Lo, within a manger lies
>   He who built the starry skies,
> He who, throned in height sublime,
>   Sits amid the cherubim.
>
> Sacred Infant, all divine,
>   What a tender love was Thine,
> Thus to come from highest bliss
>   Down to such a world as this.[2]

Yes, '*Down* to such a world as this'!

Of course it takes John's entire Gospel to explain to us how the Word stooped to conquer sin and death and Satan through his death and resurrection. But here, right at the start, John is telling us what he himself experienced and what he wants us to experience too. Although John was spiritually bankrupt, the Lord Jesus had embraced him and said to him, 'John, you are loved by me; I receive you, now you receive me.' And so he adds:

---

[1] John 1:14.
[2] From the hymn by Edward Caswall (1814–78), 'See! In yonder manger low'.

To all who did receive him, who believed in his name,
he gave the right to become children of God, who were
born, not of blood, nor of the will of the flesh nor of the
will of man, but of God ... we have seen his glory ... And
from his fullness we have all received, grace upon grace.
For ... grace and truth came through Jesus Christ.[1]

Two witnesses

If you re-read the Prologue to John's Gospel[2] you may
notice something interesting. What a modern writer would
probably put in a footnote John places within the text – a
brief comment in which he introduces John the Baptist.[3]

Since the next section in the Gospel is about John the
Baptist,[4] why did John not wait to introduce him later?

John's Gospel portrays Jesus as being on trial. In Jewish
law two witnesses were required to establish the authen-
ticity of their testimony.[5] Throughout the Gospel John
records the testimony given to Jesus by various witnesses. This climaxes in Jesus telling the apostles that together
with the Holy Spirit they would be his chief witnesses.[6]
But here, right at the beginning of the Gospel, before he
calls any other witnesses, he is telling us that there are
already two.

[1] John 1:12-14, 16-17.
[2] That is, John 1:1-18.
[3] John 1:6-8.
[4] John 1:19-37.
[5] Deuteronomy 17:6; 19:15.
[6] John 15:26-27; 20:21-23.

The first on the scene is John the Baptist. He 'came as a witness, to bear witness about the light'.[1] His testimony is 'Behold, the Lamb of God, who takes away the sin of the world.'[2]

The second witness is John the Gospel writer. His book closes with these words: 'This is the disciple who is bearing witness about these things, and who has written these things, and we know that his testimony is true.'[3]

The truth about Jesus is thus established in the mouths of two witnesses.

What John the author does here at the beginning of the Gospel is marvellous even from a literary point of view. He shows us two Johns – and both of them are pointing to the Lord Jesus. John the Apostle is saying: 'Do you see his glory?' John the Baptist is saying: 'Do you see the Lamb of God who takes away the sins of the world?'[4] They are both saying essentially the same thing. The place where we most clearly see the glory of God is in the way the Word became flesh and died for our sins as the Lamb of God.

As youngsters we used to sing a song that captures this very simply:

> There's a way back to God
>   from the dark paths of sin;
> There's a door that is open
>   and you may go in;
> At Calvary's cross is where you begin
>   when you come as a sinner to Jesus.

[1] John 1:7.
[2] John 1:15, 29.
[3] John 21:24.
[4] John 1:29.

This is John's basic message. When we grasp it and turn from spiritual darkness to the Light of the world, trusting in the one who is the Word made flesh, we are able to say:

I saw his glory and received him, and was given the right to become a child of God.

I was reborn, not by my own natural will, or because my family or friends willed it, but because God willed it.

And now I can call him 'Abba, Father!'[1]

Children of God?

Have you ever instinctively called God 'Father'? Yes, in church services or perhaps in private you have recited the Lord's Prayer with its opening words 'Our Father ...' But apart from that, it may be you have never *instinctively* called God 'Father'. Indeed, perhaps you realise that you simply don't have that instinct.

John is explaining to us how we can have it.

Our basic problem is this: whatever our birth family, we are by nature spiritual orphans, not knowing where home really is. We are spiritually dead, floating downstream with the world.[2] John is telling us where to go – to the Word made flesh – and to pray:

Lord Jesus, you are the Word made flesh; speak to my heart.

You are the Lamb of God who has taken away the sin of the world. I ask you to take away my sin.

[1] John 1:14; Romans 8:14-17.
[2] Ephesians 2:1-3.

Lord Jesus, you can bring me home to the Father.

Help me to receive you so that I too may be a child of God.

Lord, show me your glory.

The **true** *meaning of Christmas?*

When I was a child, Christmas seemed to die every year by bedtime on December 25th. The anticipation seemed long; the realisation all too brief. I even tried wrapping up my presents again and opening them the following day. But my childhood disappointment could not be relieved. It was gone for another whole year.

I know now why that was true for me, as it is for every child. It was because 'the true meaning of Christmas' eluded me. In that sense Christmas never did really 'happen'. I was looking in the wrong direction for the wrong things instead of in the right direction for Jesus.

The truth is, Christmas is not coming. It *has* come. The Word already has been made flesh. He already has lived, bled, died, and risen again for us. Now all that remains is to receive *him*. For Jesus Christ *himself* is the meaning of Christmas.

Have you received Christ? One of the ways you will know that you have is this: you will begin to call God 'Heavenly Father'.

Why not put this book aside, and do that now?

Lord God, you sent your Son from the heights of heaven to the depths of earth for us.

I have begun to see the ugliness of my sin in the light of his beauty.

I know I deserve only your judgment.

Lord, I want Jesus the Lamb of God to be the Saviour who takes away my sins. I ask you to forgive me, and to enable me to turn away from sin and begin to live for him.

Thank you, Lord, for your promise that if I seek you I will find you, and if I knock the door will be opened, no matter how sinful I have been.

Father, I confess now that I have turned from you in my sin. I need forgiveness and new life from your Son. Help me to receive him and to discover what it means to be forgiven and to become one of your own children.

I pray this in Jesus' name. Amen.

It would be easy to feel that once we have understood the Prologue to John's Gospel there is not much more we can learn about the coming of Christ. But in our next chapter we will discover that there is an inside story still to be told.

3

The Inside Story

Many passages in the Bible reflect on the coming of Christ.

The Old Testament *prophecies* look forward to Jesus' birth and life, and on occasion to his death and resurrection.

The Gospels contain *narrative descriptions* of what actually happened. Both Matthew and Luke devote two chapters of their Gospels to the events that surrounded the birth of Jesus.

Then various passages in the Epistles provide *expositions* of the meaning of Jesus' birth within the context of his life, death, and resurrection. For example:

> God has done what the law, weakened by the flesh, could not do. By sending his own Son in the likeness of sinful flesh and for sin, he condemned sin in the flesh, in order that the righteous requirement of the law might be fulfilled in us, who walk not according to the flesh but according to the Spirit.[1]

[1] Romans 8:3-4.

You know the grace of our Lord Jesus Christ, that though he was rich, yet for your sake he became poor, so that you by his poverty might become rich.[1]

When the fullness of time had come, God sent forth his Son, born of woman, born under the law, to redeem those who were under the law.[2]

Christ Jesus came into the world to save sinners.[3]

The reason the Son of God appeared was to destroy the works of the devil.[4]

Since therefore the children share in flesh and blood, he himself likewise partook of the same things, that through death he might destroy the one who has the power of death, that is, the devil, and deliver all those who through fear of death were subject to lifelong slavery.[5]

A Mount Everest

There is one passage in the New Testament, however, that rises up like Mount Everest in the Himalayas, or the Matterhorn in the Swiss Alps. It tells Jesus' story, but not from the viewpoint of observers. Its perspective is heavenly rather than earthly, supernatural rather than natural, divine rather than human, and internal rather than external. None

---

[1] 2 Corinthians 8:9.
[2] Galatians 4:4-5.
[3] 1 Timothy 1:15.
[4] 1 John 3:8.
[5] Hebrews 2:14-15.

of the familiar participants appears. Mary and Joseph, shepherds and wise men are all absent. In fact its point of view is that of the Father and the Son. It is therefore a bold, even a daring passage. It opens a window into the mindset of Christ himself. It tells the inside story of Christmas.

Here is the passage:

> Christ Jesus,
> … though he was in the form of God,
> did not count equality with God
> a thing to be grasped,
> but
> emptied himself,
> by taking the form of a servant,
> being born in the likeness of men.
>
> And being found in human form,
> he humbled himself
> by becoming obedient to the point of death,
> even death on a cross.
>
> Therefore God has highly exalted him
> and bestowed on him the name
> that is above every name,
> so that at the name of Jesus
> every knee should bow,
> in heaven and on earth and under the earth,
> and every tongue confess
> that Jesus Christ is Lord,
> to the glory of God the Father.[1]

These words have such a rhythmical quality that scholars have often wondered if they were originally sung

[1] Philippians 2:5-11.

as an early Christian hymn. They can very easily be set out in verse form, as I have done above. But whatever their background, they describe three different 'Mindsets' or 'Attitudes'.

The mindset of the Son

The central mindset is that of the Son:

> Though he was in the form of God,
> [he] did not count equality with God
> a thing to be grasped,
>
> but emptied himself,
> by taking the form of a servant,
> being born in the likeness of men.
>
> And being found in human form,
> he humbled himself
> by becoming obedient to the point of death,
> even death on a cross.
>
> Therefore God has highly exalted him.[1]

Notice the overarching pattern in this whole passage. It begins with Christ in glory ('in the form of God') and then descends to its nadir ('death on a cross') before turning upwards on its ascent. At this point a glorious reversal takes place, and Christ's exaltation, coronation, and world-wide dominion are described.

These words can be set out in the form of a parabola:

[1] Philippians 2:6-9.

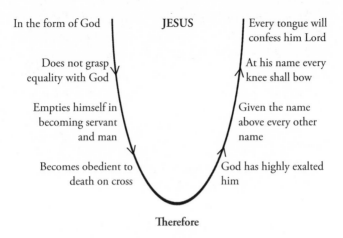

John's Prologue to his Gospel uses the same basic pattern:[1]

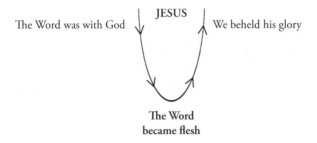

[1] John 1:1, 14.

What is remarkable in Paul's teaching in Philippians chapter 2 is that he describes *the state of mind of the Son of God.* These verses take us right inside his thinking as well as describing his external actions. He did not insist on coming into the world in a blaze of glory, but came instead in humility.

Forms

The passage begins by describing the Lord Jesus in glory. He was 'in the form of God.'

What does that mean?

The word 'form' appears three times in this passage:

1. Christ was in the 'form of God'.[1]

2. He took the 'form of a servant'.[2]

3. He came 'in human form'.[3]

In this third statement 'form' translates a Greek word (*schēma*) which means something like 'external shape'.[4] Everything about him told you he was really and truly a man.

But in the first and second statements Paul uses the Greek word *morphē*. It appears only twice in the New Testament – in these successive verses! Presumably it has the same sense in both: Christ was in the *morphē* of God

[1] Philippians 2:6.
[2] Philippians 2:7.
[3] Philippians 2:8.
[4] This is the sense in which 'appearance' in NIV should be understood. It does not imply Christ 'only appeared to be' human, but that he had a genuinely human appearance.

and when he became incarnate was also in the *morphē* of a servant or slave. Here *morphē* must mean something like 'existing as' or 'possessing the status of'.[1]

Paul is saying that Jesus was fully and truly divine. He possessed 'equality with God'. Then he came in fully and truly human form taking the status of, and existing as, a slave. The Lord of all became the servant of all.

John 'fleshes out' what this meant in his description of Jesus washing his disciples' feet in the Upper Room.[2] So this humility is not speculation on Paul's part. Jesus demonstrated it in an acted parable on the evening of his crucifixion:

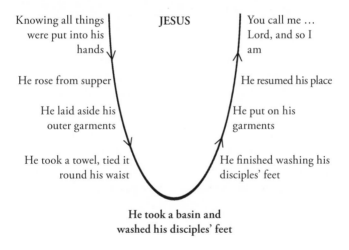

Knowing all things were put into his hands

JESUS

You call me … Lord, and so I am

He rose from supper

He resumed his place

He laid aside his outer garments

He put on his garments

He took a towel, tied it round his waist

He finished washing his disciples' feet

He took a basin and washed his disciples' feet

---

[1] Thus NIV translates: 'in very nature'.
[2] John 13:1-17.

What was going on in the mind of the Son of God when he did this? 'He did not count equality with God a thing to be grasped.'[1]

'A thing to be grasped' could refer to:

(1) 'Something I don't have, but want, and I am prepared to snatch it.'

Or:

(2) 'Something I have, but I don't feel the need to hold on tight to it and insist on expressing it, or appeal to it, in order to make myself an exception.'

In the light of what Paul writes here we can rule out interpretation (1). Christ was, after all, already in the form of God. Equality with God was something he already possessed, not something he needed to gain.

So meaning (2) fits much better. Jesus was in the form of God. He is God – God the Son. But he did not insist on receiving dignity commensurate with his identity, or appeal to his divine status as a reason why he should not humble himself or taste humiliation. Christ was in the form of God, but he did not close his fist tightly around his prerogatives as the Lord of glory and say, 'I must always have my status recognised.' He did not 'stand on his rights'.

But if this is what he did *not* think or do, what did he actually do?

Instead of gripping tightly onto, and insisting he should receive, all the visible privileges and accolades of his deity,

[1] Philippians 2:6.

the Son of God came willingly into this world of sin, and pain, and sorrow, and death. 'He made himself nothing.'

We might put it like this:

> Jesus, God's Son did not hold tightly to and insist on his prerogatives as God and say 'I will never allow myself to experience anything except what is appropriate to me as the very Son of God.' No, he came 'empty-handed' into our world.

He did that quite literally.

Imagine that the technology of the twenty-first century had been available in the first century. It would have been possible for Mary and Joseph to have seen the embryonic form of the Lord Jesus Christ in the now well-recognised fetal position, wholly dependent, lying in the darkness of his mother's womb. He came from the burning light of glory into the confined space of the body of a young woman in her teens. He brought nothing with him except himself; he came empty-handed.

Emptying himself

He 'made himself nothing'.[1] What does this mean?

The three parallel statements that follow explain it:

- taking the form of a servant

- being found in human form

- he humbled himself

He stepped into a lowly position. In doing so he emptied himself, rather than fill himself with all those external

---

[1] Philippians 2:7, AV (KJV) and ESV (Anglicised).

expressions of his deity that were his by nature and by right. Instead of receiving accolades from his subjects he came to share their weakness.

Paul's verb (*kenoō*) means 'to empty'. But he does not mean that in the incarnation Christ divested himself of his deity. When we speak of people 'emptying themselves' we do not mean they cease to be what they were. We mean they poured themselves out for us. Rather than cease to be themselves they reveal the deepest truth about themselves. God's Son did not empty himself of his divine nature, as though he gave up being God for three decades. No, Paul may actually be alluding to words used by the prophet Isaiah in his description of the coming Suffering Servant: 'He poured out his soul to death.'[1]

This is explained in a series of steps:

Step one: not grasping.

Step two: emptying himself.

Step three: being found in human form as a slave, he stooped down even lower: he humbled himself, by becoming obedient to the point of death.
And lower still: even death on a cross.

Scholars have suggested that if these words did constitute an early hymn this last statement ('even death on a cross') breaks up the pattern of the verses. It functions as a parenthesis, a few words of commentary further explaining Jesus' state of humiliation. But it is not a casual parenthesis. Paul is reminding us of the particular kind of

[1] Isaiah 53:12.

death Jesus died – that of a criminal. Worse, it was death by crucifixion.

A sense of horror surely gripped him here.

Death on a cross

You do not need to have lived in the first century in order to shudder at the words 'even death on a cross'. But they must have been loaded with special revulsion for Paul.

For one thing, Paul was a Roman citizen.[1] The word 'cross' (and its family of nouns and verbs 'crucifixion, crucify') was regarded as an obscenity in first-century Rome. A hundred years or so before Paul wrote these words the Roman orator Cicero famously stated in a speech to the Senate:

> The very mention of the cross should be far removed not
> only from a Roman citizen's body, but from his mind,
> his eyes, his ears.[2]

Indeed the cross was regarded as such an obscenity that if a sentence of death by crucifixion was pronounced, the manner of the execution was never mentioned.

But Paul held dual citizenship. He was indeed a Roman citizen; but first and foremost he was a Jew. He must therefore have felt an added horror. Indeed the way he refers to the cross makes clear that it was not its political but its theological significance that was so appalling to him.

In his earlier days it was partly this that must have made it impossible for Saul of Tarsus to believe that Jesus

---

[1] See Acts 16:37; 22:22-29.
[2] Cicero, *Pro Rabirio Postumo*, V. 16.

could be the promised Messiah. For it was written in the Scriptures that the one who hangs on a tree is cursed by God.[1]

Only later did Paul realise that the curse Jesus bore was not for himself but for him. Then he was able to say that this took place so that the blessing promised to Abraham might be fulfilled.[2]

When Paul spoke or wrote about the cross he was thinking about what the Lord Jesus accomplished for our salvation. That is not absent from his mind here.[3] But his focus is not so much on what the cross means *to us* but on what it meant *for Jesus* as the Son of God. He came from heaven's highest glory to the Roman Empire's greatest obscenity and the Bible's deepest ignominy. Such is his love for us.

In these ways Paul takes us inside the mind of Christ.

But there is more –

The mindset of the Father

Paul's letters are frequently punctuated by the word 'therefore'.[4] It suggests a logical connection between two things. Here the connection is as follows:

[1] Deuteronomy 21:23.

[2] Paul reflects on this in Galatians 3:13. This also lies behind Paul's comments in 1 Corinthians 1:21-25.

[3] A few verses later on he urges us to 'work out' this 'salvation', *i.e. not* 'work for salvation' but *rather* work it out into every area of life and in the fellowship of the church. See Philippians 2:12-13.

[4] In some modern translations (operating on the 'dynamic equivalence' principle – in English we tend not to speak using 'therefore' so frequently), this connective term is unfortunately sometimes omitted.

The Son:

>>> willingly humbled himself

> *and*

>>> experienced the humiliation of the cross

therefore

The Father:

>>> ended the humiliation

> *and*

>>> exalted his Son

Jesus knew that his Father always loved him. Within this bond of love there was a particular moment when the Father's love came to full expression. That moment was when Jesus died on the cross, as our sin-bearer at Calvary. He knew that it was 'For this reason the Father loves me, because I lay down my life that I may take it up again.'[1]

Three-stage exaltation

Paul described the self-humbling of the Son in three stages:

1. He did not count equality with God a thing to be grasped.

2. He made himself nothing, taking the form of a servant.

3. Being found in human form he humbled himself to death, even death on a cross.

Now he similarly describes his exaltation and glory in three stages.

[1] John 10:17.

Stage 1: God the Father has highly exalted his Son, and has raised him up to the position of highest honour at his right hand.

This is an all-encompassing statement, an abbreviation for Jesus' resurrection (God 'raised him up, loosing the pangs of death'[1]), his ascension (he was raised up into heaven[2]), and his exaltation (he has been 'exalted at the right hand of God'[3]). His heavenly coronation has now been celebrated visibly by the outpouring of the Spirit on the Day of Pentecost. As Peter explained: 'Being therefore exalted at the right hand of God, and having received from the Father the promise of the Holy Spirit, he has poured out this that you yourselves are seeing and hearing.'[4]

Stage 2: God the Father has given his incarnate Son the name that is above every name.

What is this name above every name?

In his humiliation God's Son had been given the name 'Jesus' in keeping with the angel's command to Joseph: 'You shall call his name Jesus, for he will save his people from their sins.'[5]

This name that Jesus bore in his humiliation he will continue to bear in his exaltation. At his ascension a second angelic announcement was made: 'This Jesus … will come [*i.e.* return] in the same way as you saw him go

[1] Acts 2:24.
[2] Acts 1:9-11.
[3] Acts 2:33.
[4] Acts 2:33.
[5] Matthew 1:21.

into heaven.'[1] He is still 'Jesus'. He is 'the same yesterday and today and forever'.[2] But now he is the 'Lord Jesus' – all authority in heaven and earth is his.[3]

Simon Peter emphasised this on the Day of Pentecost: 'Let all the house of Israel therefore know for certain that God has made him both Lord and Christ, this Jesus whom you crucified.'[4] This was the climax of the first Christian sermon. It also became the earliest Christian confession. *Iēsous Kurios!* Jesus is the same; but now *Jesus is Lord*.

These words are music to Christians' ears. Our Lord was condemned and humiliated; but now his Father has vindicated and exalted him. He has proclaimed throughout the ranks of heaven's angels, to all the redeemed around his throne, and to the powers of darkness:

> This my Son was dead, and is alive again.[5] I now exalt him to my right hand. All authority in heaven and on earth is his! Now, when he asks me, the nations will be his inheritance and the ends of the earth his possession![6]

The promise has come true: 'I will divide him a portion with the many, and he shall divide the spoil with the strong.'[7]

Stage 3: God the Father has decreed that 'at the name of Jesus every knee should bow, in heaven and on earth

---

[1] Acts 1:11.

[2] Hebrews 13:8. That is 'yesterday' (during his ministry), 'today' (in the present time), and 'forever' (for all eternity).

[3] Matthew 28:18.

[4] Acts 2:36.

[5] Luke 15:24.

[6] Cf. Matthew 28:18-20; Psalm 2:8.

[7] Isaiah 53:12.

and under the earth, and every tongue confess that Jesus Christ is Lord, to the glory of God the Father.'[1]

This third stage of his exaltation has already begun. Already the name 'Jesus' evokes in many millions of Christians an instinct to kneel before him as their Saviour and Lord. Every day, from sunrise in the East to sunset in the West, from morning in the South until evening in the North, knees bow before him, and tongues confess that 'Jesus Christ is Lord.'

In some parts of the world simply being identified with the name of Jesus demands a price that is great indeed.[2] Yet still men and women, young people, boys and girls come to faith in him as their Saviour and confess him as their Lord. There are more Christians in the world than at any time in history. Millions of knees are already bowing to Christ today. But one day *every knee* will bow, and *every tongue* will confess – whether willingly and with joy, or unwillingly and with bitter regret – that Jesus Christ is Lord to the glory of God the Father.

So Paul's words give us an insight not only into the mind of the Son, but now also into the mind of the Father. His greatest desire is to see his Son exalted. All the more so (if we may so speak) because he has seen his Son in his humility and humiliation. For that reason he has given

[1] Philippians 2:10-11.

[2] As I write these words *The Times* publishes a harrowing photograph of Christians being led along a shoreline to be executed by Islamic militants. What had been hidden from the Western public for many years – the fact that perhaps more people were killed because of the name of Jesus in the twentieth century than in all other centuries combined – is now displayed prominently in the media.

him – the Incarnate One – the name above every other name.

Only one way?

We should not fail to see an obvious implication of this – however counter-cultural it may seem to be.

The Father designed the way of salvation, involving the terrible humiliation and suffering of the crucifixion of his Son. In Gethsemane his Son asked that, if at all possible, there might be another way to save us.[1] Since there was none, *there can be no other way of salvation.*

Imagine you make a great sacrifice for someone else – a sacrifice that costs you everything you have. Why would you do that? Only because *there was no other way.* If that is true of any sacrifice we might make, how much more of the sacrifice of God's own and only Son! We dare not imagine that we can stand before the Father on the last day and say, 'Yes, I knew about the way of salvation you devised in your Son, but I preferred to create my own way instead.' If the Father found no other way, then *there is no other way.*

Considering these two mindsets – of the Son and of the Father – brings us to the end of this marvellous 'Christ hymn'. But – paradoxically – it is only when we get to the *conclusion* of it that we see the full significance of Paul's *introduction* to it. For there are not only *two* mindsets in this passage, but *three*. And the third is the mindset that we are to have! For Paul introduced the entire passage with the words, 'Have this mind among yourselves …'[2]

[1] As Jesus did ask in Gethsemane: Matthew 26:39; Mark 14:36.
[2] Philippians 2:5.

Our mindset?

All along Paul has had three responses in view:

- The response of the Son to his Father's will for him – he humbled himself;

- The response of the Father to his Son's obedience to him – he exalted him;

and

- The response we are to make to what the Son and the Father together have done for us.

Why does Paul include these eloquent words in his letter to the Philippians? He tells us: 'I want you to see the transformation that the incarnation of Christ produces in those who belong to him.'

What difference does the gospel make?

It makes a difference to everything.

Paul limits himself here to the difference it makes in our attitude to others. But he is not giving us a lecture, telling us to love others more. We already know we ought to do that, and lecturing us on it can never effect it. Rather the gospel of Christ empowers this transformation in us. We don't work it *up*. No, we are to work it *out* – 'work out your own salvation … for it is God who works in you …'[1] But the gospel works its way out of us *only once it has worked its way into us*.

How does this happen?

---

[1] Philippians 2:12-13.

When we come to trust in Christ we are united to him.[1] We begin to become like him. This transformation takes place because he gives us new life through a new birth. We come to share his mindset – the mindset 'which is yours in Christ Jesus'.[2] The Spirit of Christ begins to produce it in us when our minds are renewed by the gospel.[3]

And what is the change that takes place? We begin to count others as more significant than ourselves.[4]

This is what the Christmas gospel does. Or better, this is what the Christ of Christmas does. But he does so only when we discover the true meaning of Christmas.

We can all look around and point to some people and say, 'He/she is more important than I am.' But that is not what Paul is saying, is it? That would make no sense. For one thing, there was nobody Jesus could 'count more important' than himself in that sense. No, Jesus counted *more important to himself* people who were actually *less important than himself*. And that is what he reproduces in Christians.

This is why there is something about being with Jesus' people that is very different from being with any other group of people in the world. The mindset of Christ is, at least in miniature, reproduced in the mindset of believers. Among real Christians we see in flesh and blood terms what Paul meant when he wrote,

[1] The most frequent and dominant description Paul uses of the Christian is that he or she is someone 'in Christ'.

[2] Philippians 2:5.

[3] Romans 12:2.

[4] Philippians 2:3.

In humility count others more significant than yourselves. Let each of you look not only to his own interests,
but also to the interests of others. Have this mind among
yourselves, *which is yours in Christ Jesus.*[1]

Illustrations

We all need help to see what this looks like. Perhaps this is
why Paul almost immediately mentions two friends whom
the Philippians also knew. They both illustrated exactly
what he was talking about.[2] God has in fact designed the
church so that this would be true for all of us. He shows us
working models of biblical truth.

When I was a seventeen-year-old university student,
I had the privilege of hearing the most distinguished
Anglican preacher of his era, John R. W. Stott, expound
Philippians 2:1-11. I can still remember his opening words.

John Stott was the son of Sir Arnold Stott, had been
head boy of the famous Rugby School in England, had
graduated with a degree in Modern Languages with an
outstanding academic record, was a widely published
author, an internationally famous preacher, a chaplain to
the Queen, and spoke in a manner that was distinctive of
Rugby and Cambridge graduates! I, in marked contrast,
was the son of parents whose formal education had ended
around the age of fourteen, knew nobody in my family
tree who had ever gone to a university, and was in the first
few weeks of my degree course.

[1] Philippians 2:3-5.
[2] Timothy and Epaphroditus. Philippians 2:19-30.

He began his address by asking us a question, pausing for our answers.

My native shyness accelerated into top paralytic gear. There was no likelihood of me calling out an answer (although I can still impersonate his!).

Six years later, and now a young Presbyterian minister, I served as his 'minder' for three days when he came to speak at a ministers' conference in our church – driving him around Glasgow in a little white Austin Mini!

Eleven years further on, having had no contact with him in the intervening period, I unexpectedly received a warm and gracious letter from John Stott. He still remembered my wife's name. He had been praying for us throughout these years. That was the measure of the man.

I suspect almost everyone who heard John Stott preach, certainly every minister, imagined that he had never missed a beat in preaching, never stuttered, never used the wrong word, never packed a paragraph with 'ers' or 'ums', never lost the place, and never lacked crystal clarity. His mind seemed to be kept in a perpetually spring-cleaned condition.

Thereafter our lives occasionally intertwined. Then, in the 1990s, when Dr Stott was in his eighties, and had experienced some ill health, on each occasion I heard him preach he seemed to experience a TIA (Transient Ischaemic Attack, popularly known as 'a mini-stroke'). For a few moments the sentences would simply cease flowing. He would pause and with good humour reassure us that he would be able to continue, and then – did it seem like an eternity, standing exposed to the gaze of as many as a thousand fellow preachers who had formerly admired his clarity? – the mental engine would restart and the words would flow again.

I wondered what this felt like for him *on the inside*. This was a world to which he seemed to have been a life-long stranger. But now here was eloquence silenced, power weakened, humility humiliated.[1]

For me these occasions always caused a flashback – to the room in which I had first heard him read the words:

> Have this mind … which is yours in Christ Jesus,
> who …
> made himself nothing,
> taking the form of a servant,
> found in human fashion,
> he humbled himself …

It felt like an acted parable. Yes, it was only a fragmentary reflection; yet it reminded me of his exposition of the downward steps of our Saviour to Bethlehem and Calvary. But in Jesus' experience it was not a self-confessed sinful and frail man tasting an unwelcome weakness, in order to serve others. No, in the Saviour's case it was the Lord of glory being willing to taste abject shame for the sake of sinners.

This is the mind of Christ. It is ours in union with him. Paul urges us to let it work its way out into our individual lives and into the fellowship of the church to which we belong. How different church would be if this were to become true!

[1] John Stott's final public address was given at the Keswick Convention on July 17, 2007 on the theme of becoming more like Christ. He died on July 27, 2011.

We do not have such a mindset by nature, do we? If you think you do, others will be able to provide you with opportunities to prove that you have been deceiving yourself, by introducing you to a stream of difficult, abrasive, irritating, mean, nasty and demeaning people. Meeting them will immediately help you to realise that you do not naturally count others more important than yourself!

No, we do not naturally have this grace.

How then do we get it? Paul tells us: 'Let this mind be in you *which you have in Christ Jesus*.' We have it 'in Christ Jesus'.

We therefore have it only *when Christ Jesus has become ours*.

God's Son came from highest heaven to suffer death on a cross for my salvation. As I welcome him as my Saviour and Lord, turning away from sin, I receive the very same Christ who humbled and emptied himself and became obedient to the death of the cross. I cannot receive the exalted Lord Jesus without embracing the crucified Jesus. And when I embrace him in faith as he is offered to me freely in the gospel, I begin to experience what the Father's highest desire for me is – that through faith in Christ I should share his devotion to, and love for, his Son. Then, in turn, he will pursue his passion for me: to make me more and more like Jesus so that I too will count others as more important than myself.

If that were to be true of you it would not be long before it was obvious that you understood the *true* meaning of Christmas!

But we are slowly discovering that there are hidden depths to this meaning, and we have yet more of them to explore.

4

Immanuel

M ost of us are influenced to some degree or another by the popular music of our own generation. The music we listen to as teenagers expresses the cultural atmosphere in which we grow up. It is the background music to the narrative of our self-discovery. If you have ever sat with a group of people in the generation above your own, and a popular song from their teenage years is mentioned, the conversation usually develops into a series of 'Do you remember this one …?' This begins to stimulate recollections of the songs of their youth (most of which are unknown to you). Yet it is likely that some of the group know hardly any popular songs recorded since then!

If you belong to the generation of the so-called 'Baby Boomers' – unless you have lived a sheltered life – the names of Paul Simon and Art Garfunkel will feature somewhere in your musical memory banks.

One morning in late 1971 I was house-sitting for my older brother. I noticed the Simon and Garfunkel LP

Parsley, Sage, Rosemary and Thyme[1] in his record collection. Never having heard it, I played it on his music centre while I read.

The music retreated into the background as I became engrossed in my book until it became simply that – *background* music. But suddenly I was jolted out of my reading. Something seemed to have gone badly wrong with my brother's (expensive) music centre – damage for which I might be held responsible; either that or I was losing my mind!

Here I was in Glasgow, Scotland, listening to Simon and Garfunkel; but I was hearing an American voice, at first almost imperceptibly, reading a news bulletin:

> The recent fight in the House of Representatives was over the open housing section of the Civil Rights Bill.
>
> Brought traditional enemies together but left the defenders of the measure without the votes of their strongest supporters.
>
> President Johnson originally proposed an outright ban covering discrimination by everyone for every type of housing but it had no chance from the start and everyone in Congress knew it.
>
> A compromise was painfully worked out by the House Judiciary Committee.
>
> In Los Angeles today comedian Lenny Bruce died of what was believed to be an overdose of narcotics.
>
> Bruce was 42 years old.
>
> Dr Martin Luther King says he does not intend to cancel plans for an open housing march Sunday in the Chicago suburb of Cicero.

[1] Named from words in the first track, 'Are you going to Scarborough Fair?'

Cook County Sheriff Richard Ogleby asked King to call off the march and the police in Cicero said they would ask the National Guard to be called out if it is held.

King, now in Atlanta, Georgia, plans to return to Chicago Tuesday.

In Chicago, Richard Speck, accused murderer of nine student nurses, was brought before a grand jury today for indictment.

The nurses were found stabbed and strangled in their Chicago apartment.

In Washington the atmosphere was tense today as a special subcommittee of the House Committee on Un-American Activities continued its probe into anti-Vietnam War protests.

Demonstrators were forcibly evicted from the hearings when they began chanting anti-war slogans.

Former Vice-President Nixon says that unless there is a substantial increase in the present war effort in Vietnam, the U.S. should look forward to five more years of war.

In a speech before the Convention of the Veterans of Foreign Wars in New York, Nixon also said opposition to the war in this country is the greatest single weapon working against the U.S.

That's the 7 o'clock edition of the news.

Good night.

If you know this recording, you will also know that these words were 'voiced over' or perhaps better 'voiced into' Simon and Garfunkel singing the German Christmas Carol 'Silent Night':

Silent night! holy night!
All is calm, all is bright
Round yon virgin mother and Child,
Holy Infant so tender and mild,
Sleep in heavenly peace!
Sleep in heavenly peace!

The track is, of course, entitled '7 O'Clock News/Silent Night.' But I had not read the play list. The impact was therefore, if anything, all the greater.

The recording belonged to the 'protest song' genre. The whole point of it lay in the stark contrast between the words of the newscaster and those of a carol sung the world over each Christmas, its tune played in countless department stores, even in openly secular countries – perhaps unthinkingly, perhaps sentimentally, perhaps, in Simon and Garfunkel's view, even hypocritically. It was a powerful statement about a world *without* 'heavenly peace'.

Leaving aside for the moment the somewhat romanticised view of Jesus' birth and infancy expressed in the carol, and the false assumption that Christ came to bring 'peace in our time',[1] the Simon and Garfunkel recording

---

[1] It is becoming increasingly clear in the Western world (*e.g.* in 'Letters to the Editor' and even in the leader columns of our newspapers) that our culture has very little understanding of what the Christian faith really is, and has reduced it to a kind of religious lowest common denominator that we should (in some ill-defined way) 'love each other, not judge others, be tolerant, and do your best'. This sits uncomfortably with the teaching of Jesus, as a cursory reading of the Gospels would show, not least the 'much loved' Sermon on the Mount in Matthew 5:1 – 7:29. Indeed Jesus made it clear that the result of his coming would be division. His disciples would experience tribulation. Only in him would they find peace. See Matthew 10:34; John 16:33.

raises a question: Is the Christmas message just an illusion, an annual expression of communal wishful thinking?

No doubt Christmas illusions do need to be destroyed in many people's minds. Santa Claus is not Jesus Christ any more than the Easter Bunny is the resurrection. The message of Christ's coming does not offer us the hope of international peace that so many see in it. Only the naïve think that the constantly repeated (and sincere?) aspiration of today's television and media personalities' Christmas wish for 'world peace' is anything more than illusion. Peace can come only where there is no more sin. War *without* cannot cease so long as there is war *within*. As Jesus indicated, wars, conflicts, and rumours of both will be with us, along with the poor, until the end.[1] 'World peace' in this secular sense is not the meaning of Christmas.

Enter Immanuel

In a day not dissimilar from our own the prophet Isaiah announced that Immanuel would come:

> Behold, the virgin shall conceive and bear a son, and shall call his name Immanuel.[2]

It is easy for us to lose sight of the fact that 'Immanuel', 'God with us', was one of the most familiar and important convictions of the Old Testament. It lay at the heart of the promise God gave to Jacob;[3] and was a key to help Moses to understand the significance of God's name Yahweh – he

---

[1] Matthew 24:6; John 12:8.
[2] Isaiah 7:14.
[3] Genesis 28:15.

would be God-with-him.[1] Think of the comfort of which David speaks in probably the most famous words in the Old Testament, perhaps even in the whole Bible:

> Even though I walk through the valley of
> the shadow of death,
> I will fear no evil,
> for you are with me.[2]

So why was Isaiah's prophecy so remarkable? Because he said that his prophecy was going to be fulfilled in a child. The promise points forward to the day when 'the Word became flesh and dwelt among us'. For he is Immanuel – God with us.

Virgin born

Isaiah indicated that the child Immanuel would be conceived in the womb of a virgin.

This was the promise Matthew said was fulfilled in the coming of Jesus.[3] Paradoxically some scholars accuse Matthew of shaping his story to fulfil this prophecy, while others accuse him of misunderstanding the prophecy since the Hebrew word for a virgin refers to 'a young woman of marriageable age'.

But in Isaiah's culture a 'young woman of marriageable age' was assumed to be a virgin. And given the pre-understanding of 'Immanuel, God with us' the unique nature of his conception and birth is wholly in keeping with the

[1] Exodus 3:12.
[2] Psalm 23:4. See also Psalm 46:7; 91:15; Isaiah 41:10; 43:2.
[3] Matthew 1:23.

astonishing revelation that Yahweh, Immanuel, God with us, has planned to enter his world in human form.

Amazing though the virgin birth is – or more fundamentally the virgin *conception* – it is altogether appropriate. If the eternal Word became flesh for our sake, by what other means would we expect this to happen? For the Saviour needs to have flesh and blood like ourselves and yet at the same time be sent from God. We may not be able to understand *how* the Spirit of God brought about the conception of Jesus in the womb of the Virgin Mary. But it is altogether consistent and indeed logical to believe that the God who created all things out of nothing is capable of bringing his Son into the world in this way.

But who was this child, Immanuel, to be?

Isaiah himself must have wondered. Neither he nor his fellow writing prophets knew exactly how their prophecies would be fulfilled. Rather, long before the wise men were searching for Christ they were doing the same:

> The prophets … searched and inquired carefully, inquiring what person or time the Spirit of Christ in them was indicating when he predicted the sufferings of Christ and the subsequent glories.[1]

More light

Was it in response to Isaiah's quest for more light that the Lord soon revealed additional ways to pronounce 'Immanuel'? He later spells it out for us by means of four names:

[1] 1 Peter 1:10-11.

For to us a child is born,
  to us a son is given;
and the government shall be upon his shoulder,
  and his name shall be called
Wonderful Counsellor, Mighty God,
  Everlasting Father, Prince of Peace.[1]

But now Isaiah sees this child appear against a very dark backcloth indeed: people peering through the gloom as they walk in darkness, bowed beneath a heavy yoke, beaten by an oppressor's rod, haunted by the sound of the marching boots of enemy warriors. Yet deliverance comes:

The people who walked in darkness
  have seen a great light;
those who dwelt in a land of deep darkness …

For the yoke of his burden,
  and the staff for his shoulder,
  the rod of his oppressor,
  you have broken as on the day of Midian.
For every boot of the tramping warrior in battle tumult
  and every garment rolled in blood
  will be burned as fuel for the fire.
For to us a child is born …[2]

As his prophecies unfolded, it became clearer to Isaiah that his vision of the people's geographical exile and bondage in Babylon was only the outer shell of a deeper exile and bondage in sin. For this no political deliverer – such as Cyrus, the Persian king who would make possible the

[1] Isaiah 9:6.
[2] Isaiah 9:2, 4-6.

return from exile[1] – could possibly be adequate. Deliverance from the guilt and power of sin requires that someone make atonement for it.

So Isaiah caught sight of the coming Immanuel; he prophesied about a Wonderful Counsellor. But later still he saw another figure coming over the horizon – this time a Servant who would suffer and bear his people's guilt.[2]

Immanuel, Counsellor, Servant. Did Isaiah ever realise that these three figures would turn out to be one and the same person? Did he make the connection between 'the Prince of Peace' and 'the Servant' who would experience 'the chastisement that brought us peace'?[3] Did he see that the child to be conceived in the womb of the virgin would one day appear as 'a root out of dry ground' and be 'like a lamb that is led to the slaughter'?[4]

All three of these passages in Isaiah (in chapters 7, 9, and 52-53) are either quoted or alluded to in the New Testament as prophecies referring to Jesus.[5] From the perspective of the apostles (and presumably here they are teaching

---

[1] Isaiah 45:1-7.

[2] See Isaiah 42:1-9; 49:1-7; 50:4-11; and especially 52:13 – 53:12.

[3] Isaiah 9:6; 53:5.

[4] Isaiah 7:14; 53:2, 7.

[5] Isaiah 7:14 is quoted in Matthew 1:23, and alluded to in Luke 1:31.

Isaiah 9:1-2 is cited in Matthew 4:15-16, and Isaiah 9:2-7 is alluded to in Luke 1:78-79; 2:32-33; John 1:45; 1 Peter 2:9.

Isaiah 53 is quoted in Matthew 8:17; Luke 22:37; John 12:38; Acts 8:32-33; Romans 10:16; 1 Peter 2:22.

It is alluded to in at least the following passages: Matthew 26:63, 67; 27:12, 38; Mark 9:12; 14:60-61; Luke 23:33; 24:46; John 1:29; Acts 10:43; Romans 4:25; 5:19; 1 Corinthians 5:7; 15:3; Hebrews 9:28; 1 Peter 1:11; 2:23-24; 1 John 3:5; Revelation 5:6, 12; 13:8; 14:5.

what Jesus taught them and commanded them to teach us[1]) there can be no doubt. Isaiah's message of salvation and new life is fulfilled in Jesus Christ, and in him alone.

Jesus Immanuel is the light of the world who penetrates the darkness. He provides everything we need for our salvation.[2] He does so because he exercises a four-fold ministry as Wonderful Counsellor, Mighty God, Everlasting Father, and Prince of Peace. He is all of these things, all of the time, for all of his people. Isaiah knew much less about him than we now do. Yet he understood that *what he would do tells us a great deal about what we most need*.

Wonderful Counsellor

The term 'counsellor' has come into its own in our time. Increasingly in the modern world giving counsel has become less of the activity of a friend and more of a salaried profession. High schools, as well as colleges and universities, have student counsellors. As soon as the emergency services have handled the first hours of a tragedy, expert trauma counsellors are present. There are counselling services for the military, for financial planning, for personal lifestyle, for beauty, for becoming a more aggressive person, but also for dealing with more aggressive people (do the same people run both services?). There is counselling by psychologists and psychiatrists, there is Christian counselling and secular counselling. Fees are agreed, people become 'clients' and health insurance companies build allowances for counselling into their coverage.

---

[1] See Matthew 28:18-20, especially in the light of Luke 24:44-49 and Acts 1:1-3.

[2] John 8:12.

No one should despise the need for wise counsel. We all need direction. But increasingly the counsel people receive lacks a moral compass. The Maker's instructions and goal are no longer regarded as relevant; indeed they may be seen as harmful to the psyche. It should hardly surprise us if, despite pouring multi-millions into raising the self-esteem of our young people, the indications are that they are more lost than ever emotionally, psychologically, and spiritually.[1] When there is no moral 'magnetic north' parents, children, governments and educational systems are at the mercy of the theories of the moment. Where is wisdom to be found?

Our problem is manifold. The effects of the Fall are holistic. It has produced disorder in what Paul calls 'spirit and soul and body'.[2]

Thankfully, God in his common grace has embedded into the very structure of the world the resources that make possible the discovery of many pharmaceutical antidotes and remedies for our physical ailments. He is the ultimate source of all true medical, surgical, and psychiatric help. But if our fundamental problem is that we are in deep spiritual darkness the antidote must be spiritual light, not a pharmaceutical prescription. What we need most of all is a counsellor who will give us *light* on the ultimate causes of our condition and point us to its remedy. Only this will enable us to see who we are, where we are, the nature of

---

[1] In this context Professor Glynn Harrison has provided a perceptive analysis of the response of our culture (and various levels of government) to the crisis of identity and self-image in *The Big Ego Trip* (Nottingham: IVP, 2013).

[2] 1 Thessalonians 5:23.

our situation, and a pathway out of it. What we need most is not simply medicine to add a few years to our life, or to provide us with a better quality of life. This life will end. We need counsel that will point us to eternal life.

Isaiah recognised the true nature of our problem and saw the solution: 'The people who walked in darkness have seen a great light.'[1] Jesus Christ, the coming Immanuel, brings this light. His word shows us the truth about our condition (darkness), and brings us into its light. In his light we see light![2] He further promises that those who follow him will never walk in total darkness but will have the light of life.[3]

But where do we find his counsel?

Jesus is the Wonderful Counsellor. He promised that, in addition to his own ministry to his disciples as their *Paraklētos* or Counsellor, he would send the Holy Spirit to them to continue that ministry. As a result the apostles would come to understand who Jesus was, the significance of what he had said, and the power of what he would do in his death and resurrection.

Jesus commanded them to share that truth with us.[4] It has now been embedded in the pages of the New Testament.[5]

Paul assures us that the Scriptures have been given to us with four goals in view: God's word is 'profitable for

[1] Isaiah 9:2.
[2] Psalm 36:9.
[3] John 8:12.
[4] John 16:13 and Matthew 28:18-20.
[5] This is further explained in my *From the Mouth of God* (Edinburgh: Banner of Truth Trust, 2014), 14-16, 31-34.

teaching, for reproof, for correction, and for training in righteousness'.[1]

• **Teaching.** The teaching of Scripture gives instruction to our minds to enable us to think clearly, to see things from God's perspective, and to view our world from its true centre in God.

• **Reproof.** This inevitably leads to an awareness of how badly things have gone wrong – and we experience reproof. The light of God's truth reveals the untruth in our lives. We have fallen short of what we were meant to be – a perspective embedded in the basic New Testament word for sin (*hamartia*) – missing or falling short of the target. Since what we have fallen short of is 'the glory of God',[2] this unravelling of our true spiritual condition will be both deep and multi-dimensional.

• **Correction.** But Scripture also fills us with hope. Its light and wisdom 'correct' us – in the sense of mending us, healing us, transforming us. The word Paul uses here (*epanorthōsis*), translated 'correction', was used in the medical world for the resetting of a bone, or correcting a deformity. Just as the word of Jesus restored men and women during his Galilean ministry, so he restores, remakes, and transforms us by it still today.

• **Training.** All this has in view 'training in righteousness'. The word 'training' (*paideia*) belongs to the world of the family (*pais* is the Greek word for a child). In view here is child-training in the family – learning what it means

[1] 2 Timothy 3:16.
[2] Romans 3:23.

to be a child of God, introducing us to what it means to live as Christians who know that the heavenly Father has adopted us as his own children.

Resisting the light

We might think that people would be eager to go to the Wonderful Counsellor to receive the wisdom of his word. But it is not so. By nature we resist the strong beams of light that God's word shines into our lives.[1]

One of the strongest and most penetrating of these invasive beams is found in Paul's concentrated analysis of the human condition in Romans 1:18-32. It is one of the most politically incorrect passages in the whole of the New Testament. So much so that when a group of Christian students printed and distributed this section of Romans without indicating its source they were summoned before the governing board of their college – with a demand that the author of the tract come with them! Few things could more clearly illustrate the extent to which the word of God rebukes or convicts, gets under our skin, and exposes the truth about our situation. Sadly too the incident provides an index of the lack of knowledge of the basic documents of the Christian faith that exists today even among highly educated people.

Here is what Paul wrote:

> For the wrath of God is revealed from heaven against all ungodliness and unrighteousness of men, who by their unrighteousness suppress the truth. For what can be known about God is plain to them, because God has

[1] John 3:19-21.

shown it to them. For his invisible attributes, namely, his eternal power and divine nature, have been clearly perceived, ever since the creation of the world, in the things that have been made. So they are without excuse. For although they knew God, they did not honour him as God or give thanks to him, but they became futile in their thinking, and their foolish hearts were darkened. Claiming to be wise, they became fools, and exchanged the glory of the immortal God for images resembling mortal man and birds and animals and reptiles.

Therefore God gave them up in the lusts of their hearts to impurity, to the dishonouring of their bodies among themselves, because they exchanged the truth about God for a lie and worshiped and served the creature rather than the Creator, who is blessed forever! Amen.[1]

What is Paul saying? The darkness in which we live is the fruit of the way we suppress what we know to be true. We exchange the truth about God for a lie. We give our hearts to created things but refuse to give them to the Creator. We reverse the divine value system. Ultimately we become self-deceived and then need to encourage others to imitate and join us lest the truth expose us.[2] We repress what we cannot face, namely that deep down we are all aware of God simply because his revelation surrounds us in creation and invades us since we have all been created as his image.

The result? We pretend to ourselves and to others that all is well when in fact all is ultimately lost. How telling it

[1] Romans 1:18-25.
[2] Romans 1:32.

is that not only Paul (of Tarsus) the apostle but also Paul (Simon) the song-writer gives expression to this:

> Through the corridors of sleep
> Past the shadows dark and deep
> My mind dances and leaps in confusion.
> I don't know what is true,
> I can't touch what I feel
> And I hide behind the shield of my illusion.
> So I'll continue to continue to pretend
> My life will never end,
> And flowers never bend with the rainfall.[1]

So here is my problem: I am spiritually blind and need light; spiritually deaf and need to hear the voice of Christ calling me; I am spiritually dead and in need of new life. I need help from outside. Is there anyone out there who can help me?

Jesus Christ can! He is a Wonderful Counsellor. He not only shines light into my darkness; he tells me where more light is to be found. He is himself the light. And when he shines his light into our lives we come to life. This is his promise:

> I am the light of the world. Whoever follows me will not walk in darkness, but will have the light of life.[2]

Since those are the words that first brought me to faith, there is only one comment I would like to add to them: *True!*

---

[1] Paul Simon, 'Flowers never bend with the rainfall'.
[2] John 8:12.

5

Bad News – Good News (Immanuel Part Two)

Our school morning assembly always included a Scripture passage read by one of the senior pupils. That day it was my friend's turn. He stood up at the lectern and confidently announced the passage: 'The reading this morning is from the Gospel according to Isaiah.'

I remember feeling a wave of embarrassment sweeping over me on his behalf. Inwardly I said 'Oh John! Isaiah isn't a Gospel!'[1]

Isaiah did not write one of the four Gospels. He lived centuries before the coming of Jesus. But in one sense my friend was right. Isaiah's prophecy is a Gospel – it is full of the gospel. He may not have known the identity of the person whose coming he predicted,[2] but he certainly knew that his coming was good news.

[1] Since he will have no memory of the occasion I have changed my friend's name to protect the guilty!
[2] 1 Peter 1:10-12.

He also knew that good news implies that there is bad news.

This basic biblical principle was to be so deeply embedded in Isaiah's message that the Lord had led him to give his two sons names that would express it. One son was called Maher-shalal-hashbaz – which means 'The spoil speeds, the prey hastens'.[1] The other's name was Shear-jashub, which means 'A remnant shall return'.[2] Here was very bad news – the people would be taken into exile in Babylon. But here too was good news – some of the exiles would return to Jerusalem. Bad news, good news.

Much later on Luke would indicate that this was also the context for the birth of Jesus. Into a world in which bad news came from the Emperor's throne that Rome demanded tribute from the nations it had subjugated, angels brought good news from the throne of God that a Saviour had been born.[3]

Isaiah's good news long predated that of the Bethlehem angels. But the good news was the same: a virgin bearing a son with a significant name, Immanuel, God with us. The result, Isaiah continued, would be that

> The people who walked in darkness
>   have seen a great light;
> those who dwelt in a land of deep darkness,
>   on them has light shined.[4]

This, as he went on to explain, was because Immanuel was not the child's only name:

[1] Isaiah 8:3.
[2] Isaiah 7:3.
[3] Luke 2:1, 9-14.
[4] Isaiah 9:2.

> And his name shall be called
> Wonderful Counsellor …

We have seen how the Lord Jesus fulfilled this prophecy. He came into our darkness in order to lead us out of it. He shows us the way. He sheds light on our path.

But we have already learned that Wonderful Counsellor is not Immanuel's only additional name. The bad news is that we suffer from more than darkness, and we need more than the light of his counsel. The good news is that the Wonderful Counsellor is also called

> … Mighty God,
> Everlasting Father, Prince of Peace.

Why is this also essential to the good news of the coming of Immanuel? Is it not enough that he should be a Wonderful Counsellor?

Mighty God

I lack light. Jesus Christ gives it. But I also lack power – power of will to trust in Christ and power in my affections to love God. According to Paul's analysis I am

- Dead in trespasses and sins
- Following the course of this world
- Following the prince of the power of the air[1]

But Immanuel has all the power I need to give me life and set me free. For he is 'the *mighty* God'.

---

[1] Ephesians 2:1-2.

There is a nuance here that we can easily miss in an English translation. For the word Isaiah uses, translated 'mighty' (*gibbor*), has an undertone of the heroic. Immanuel does things in an heroic fashion.

Isaiah gives us a vivid illustration of what this means. He likens the salvation Immanuel brings to one of the great heroic moments in the history of God's people:

> For the yoke of his burden,
>> and the staff for his shoulder,
>> the rod of his oppressor,
>> you have broken *as on the day of Midian*.[1]

But what does it mean that our situation is like that of 'the day of Midian'?

The allusion is to the days described in the Book of Judges when Israel's persistent sin led to their defeat and oppression by the pagan nations around them. This serves as a dramatic parable for spiritual oppression and deliverance. Sin brings bondage. At the same time we are beaten by the demands of the law, which in this sense contains no mercy.[2] But, Isaiah says, Immanuel will break the yoke, the staff, and the rod, and set us free 'as on the day of Midian'.

---

[1] Isaiah 9:4.

[2] John Bunyan illustrates this in his vivid description of Faithful, the Pilgrim's companion, being beaten by Moses who represents the demands of the law. When asked to show mercy, he responds, 'I know not how to show mercy.' John Bunyan, *The Pilgrim's Progress*, edited with an introduction by Roger Sharrock (Harmondsworth: Penguin Books, 1965), 63.

The day of Midian

Israel had become virtually a vassal state of the Midianites and 'was brought very low'.[1] But in their need the people 'cried out for help'.

In due course God raised up Gideon, who destroyed the offensive altar of the pagan god Baal and also the idolatrous Asherah poles.[2] The Midianites, the Amalekites, and others responded by sending an army that assembled for battle in the great Valley of Jezreel. In response Gideon summoned men from Manasseh, Asher, Zebulun, and Naphtali and raised an army of 32,000.

God, however, had a different strategy:

> The LORD said to Gideon, 'The people with you are too many for me to give the Midianites into their hand …
> Now therefore proclaim in the ears of the people, saying, "Whoever is fearful and trembling, let him return home and hurry away from Mount Gilead."'[3]

'Too many'? 'Whoever is fearful and trembling, let him return home and hurry away'? What kind of military strategy was this? Gideon was left now with an army of only 10,000 troops.

The story then continues just as unexpectedly: 'And the LORD said to Gideon, "The people are still too many …"' He told him to take the remaining men down to the water to get a drink, and to send away any of them who knelt right down in order to do so.

That accounted for another 9,700 troops.

[1] Judges 6:6.
[2] Canaanite nature and fertility gods.
[3] Judges 7:2-3.

32,000 minus 22,000 minus 9,700 leaves a trimmed-down fighting force of 300 men!

Clearly there is no misprint in the Bible's record here. The Lord apparently did say that 32,000 and then 10,000 were *too many*.[1] He really did mean to whittle down the numbers. And for a reason: his plan was not to defeat the Midianites by greater numbers and superior artillery power but by a few and by weakness. The weapons Gideon was now to hand out to his men were not an ancient version of Kalashnikovs, but a bad dream, and 300 men with trumpets, empty jars, and torches!

First the Lord providentially used a Midianite soldier's dream about their defeat to create a sense of foreboding in the army. Then the sound of 300 trumpets, the noise of 300 breaking jars, the light of 300 torches, and the triumphant battle cry 'a sword for the Lord and for Gideon!' sent the Midianite army into panic and flight. In their confusion many of them killed each other. All that was left to Gideon's men was the mopping-up operation that followed with the aid of the Ephraimites.[2]

What is the point of this extended simile Isaiah employs? Ultimately this: in Jesus Christ we have a divine hero who brings us deliverance from sin, and death, and hell. He does this in an heroic fashion 'as in the day of Midian'. He comes empty-handed, in the frailty of the incarnation. And then he dies in the weakness and apparent folly of crucifixion. He even came as a 'child'. The sign to the shepherds that he was 'Christ the Lord' was that

[1] Judges 7:2, 4.
[2] The whole story makes for gripping reading. See Judges 6:28 – 7:25.

they would find him 'wrapped in swaddling cloths and lying in a manger'. What kind of 'Mighty God' is he?

This is the paradox of the Christian gospel, as Paul saw so clearly. In his day he observed that Greeks demanded impressive philosophical arguments, while Jews looked for power to be manifested in awe-inspiring signs. But he himself had come to see that in Christ's death and resurrection God demonstrates that his folly is wiser than man's wisdom and his weakness is stronger than man's strength.[1] The oppression of sin and guilt, Satan, and death are all dealt with through the cross of Christ in which he overcame the dominion of sin, bore its guilt, died our death, and in his resurrection power conquered our enemy. Folly overcame wisdom; weakness conquered strength.

So it was on the day of Midian. So it would be, Isaiah foresaw, in the days of Bethlehem and Golgotha. This too is part of the message about the child who was to be born, and therefore of the meaning of Christmas.

In this way, Isaiah notes, 'the government shall be upon his shoulder'.

Shouldering government

In the Gospel narrative only one thing ever seems to have been placed on Jesus' shoulders: the cross he was forced to carry to the place of his execution. He entered into his government by means of this tree. The early fathers of the church used to reflect on the fact that the disobedience that took place at a tree found its antidote in the obedience that took place at another tree. By his atoning death and

---

[1] 1 Corinthians 1:22-25.

justifying resurrection Christ established his kingdom. He defeated all his and our enemies. Now, through faith, we come under his government. We are set free to live for him through the weakness of the cross!

So this is where God's salvation is found – in Christ crucified and risen. In him the power of God is manifested through weakness, and the wisdom of God is demonstrated through the foolishness of the cross.

Knowing this has made it possible for believers to live the Christian life under any regime in the history of the world. While many enjoy political freedom and yet are spiritually enslaved, the gospel enables others who are in prison for the name of Jesus and confined to tiny cells to live as free men and women in Christ.

So Isaiah is looking forward to this day, when Immanuel, God with us, will win an heroic victory.

Everlasting Father

But there is more, because we need more. For we are not only in darkness and bondage, we are also homeless. We are spiritual orphans. We need a father, and we need to know that we are loved. Immanuel is such an 'Everlasting Father'.

At first sight this seems a little confusing. Christians say that God is Trinity – Father, Son, and Holy Spirit. How can he say that Immanuel, God with us, will be the Everlasting Father?

There is no ultimate contradiction here. Isaiah is not thinking about the relationships within the Trinity. His focus is on what happens when God is with us in and through Jesus Christ. Just as a king was 'father' to his nation, so the one on whose shoulders the government rests becomes our father and through him we are adopted into the family of God. Remember what John had said in his Prologue: 'To all who did receive him [Christ, the Word of God], who believed in his name, he gave the right to become children of God.'[1]

We were created to belong to God's family, to enjoy his love and care, to be satisfied in his presence, and to marvel at his wisdom. Instead our first parents rejected his wisdom, were lured into thinking meanly of his care, hid from his presence, and fell under the power of sin and shame.

Sin thus rendered us Fatherless. We may still be able to recite The Lord's Prayer,[2] but that is not necessarily the same as knowing and trusting him as our Father. Now, tragically, none of us is by nature a child of God. Like Paul – who could lay claim to all the privileges of being a faithful and devoted son of Abraham – we too were 'by nature *children of wrath, like the rest of mankind*'.[3] In this he simply echoes Jesus. He went so far as to say to some of his own countrymen who opposed him, 'If God were your Father, you would love me ... You are of your father the devil ...'[4]

---

[1] John 1:12.

[2] The prayer that Jesus taught his disciples: 'Our Father in heaven, hallowed be your name. Your kingdom come, your will be done, on earth as it is in heaven. Give us this day our daily bread, and forgive us our debts, as we also have forgiven our debtors. And lead us not into temptation, but deliver us from evil.' Matthew 6:9-13.

[3] See Ephesians 2:1-3.

[4] John 8:42, 44.

This is not the Jesus of popular imagination, and certainly not the way most people say they 'like to think about Jesus'. His unnerving message is this: 'If you do not love me you cannot be a child in God's family; you are in the family line spawned by the serpent in the Garden of Eden!'

What then?

We need to be adopted into the family of God. This can take place only through Immanuel. In him alone can we be sure of God's love for us. Only the cross can prove that love to us and give us the confidence to say: 'He who did not spare his own Son but gave him up for us all, how will he not also with him graciously give us all things?'[1]

Here Paul is echoing the words of Genesis 22 in which God describes Abraham's willingness to sacrifice his son, Isaac – the son whom he loved.[2] But while Abraham was willing not to spare his son, God was not willing for Abraham to sacrifice him. He had a more breathtaking plan – not to spare his own Son, the Son whom he loved! Why? So that through the death and resurrection of his own Son, God might bring all those who trust in him into his family. He adopts us. We become his. He reassures us of his love and care, provides for our needs, and promises to bring us all the way home.

But we discover this only in Jesus Christ.

[1] Romans 8:32.

[2] The account is found in Genesis 22:1-19. Notice especially the wording in verses 2, 12, and 16.

The prodigals' Father

Jesus' parable of the Prodigal Son can help us here. He told it to those who criticised him for welcoming sinners.[1] To that extent the father in the parable represents Jesus himself. He welcomes one particular sinner and brings him back into the family.

But there is more to this than meets the eye.

In Jesus' culture there was a ceremony in place for occasions like the return of a prodigal son. It was very different from the 'ceremony' the father in the parable arranged. It was a shunning ceremony. The wayward son would be publicly shamed. A righteous father could not welcome home such a prodigal without recriminations, could he? But in Jesus' parable the father absorbs all the prodigal's shame himself – just like Jesus.

The details here are spell-binding:

(1) The father *runs* to welcome his wayward son (dignified Jewish fathers did not *run* – especially not to welcome prodigals).

(2) The father embraces and kisses his son (instead of disowning him).

(3) The father has the best robe (presumably his own), and the ring and the shoes brought for the prodigal (wearing shoes in the family home was a prerogative of family members only).

(4) The father then – to crown it all – throws a celebratory party for him (food, singing, and dancing) – instead of shaming and shunning him.

---

[1] Luke 15:2.

Projecting the wrong way round?

Since the days of Karl Marx and Sigmund Freud (and behind them thinkers like Ludwig Feuerbach)[1] Christian faith has been accused of being no more than a form of 'projectionism'. We are used to hearing this in a popular form: 'You are a Christian simply because *you need a father-figure.* You are simply projecting your needs and creating a God who meets them. That is where all this comes from. Your faith is simply a crutch.'

From its opening page the Bible teaches us that the very reverse is the case. We do not create God as a father-figure because we need one. Rather, God the Father has created son-figures because he wants them! This is what it means to be created as his image and likeness. And it is the reason why we cannot truly be ourselves without him.

God is not a projection of our needs; we were created for him. If anything we are a 'projection' into reality created for his pleasure. How can we rest satisfied until we know

---

[1] Ludwig Feuerbach (1804–72) was a German philosopher, best known today for his book *The Essence of Christianity*, in which he expounded the idea that 'God' is simply a projection of man. In some ways he simply took to its (disastrous) logical conclusion the idea of the theologian Friedrich Schleiermacher (1768–1834) that the essence of Christian faith resides in the individual's feeling or sense of absolute dependence on God. Schleiermacher, in turn, believed he was preserving Christian faith from the assaults of Enlightenment thought which had closed off the possibility of any objective knowledge of God. While Marx ultimately reacted against aspects of Feuerbach's thought, and disagreed with him about the *causes* behind the projection of the existence of God (Feuerbach thought of it in psychological terms while Marx construed it in empirical historical terms), he shared the view that 'God' was indeed nothing more than a projection.

we are his children and until we have come once more to bear the family likeness we have lost?[1]

The tragedy of contemporary secular *humanism* at this point is precisely that it is ultimately inhumane! It demeans rather than exalts man. It has become blind to the obvious. For if we deny the Father whose image we were created to be we not only deny the truth about ourselves, but we demean ourselves. To see man as in essence simply an advanced 'naked ape' inevitably leads to a loss of dignity and real humanity. When we refuse to stay at home with the Father we waste our inheritance.

The additional tragedy is that like the prodigal we have come to think ill of the all-generous Father. We have imbibed the poison of the serpent who first insinuated that God was treating his children in a miserly fashion.[2] Thus we are a mixture of prodigal sons and elder brothers who see God as a slave master and refuse to enjoy the celebrations of his grace.[3]

So long as this is true of us we do not know what we are missing! We never come home. Or if, as often happens, we think of ourselves as 'religious', we stay at home. But like the elder brother in the parable we never go into the house.

---

[1] Genesis 1:26-28 is echoed later in Scripture, as in Genesis 5:1-3 (Adam is God's image; Seth was Adam's son, 'in his own likeness, after his image'). Clearly here the concepts of 'image', 'likeness', and 'son' are intimately related. If not quite interchangeable, they are integrated at a deep level.

[2] Genesis 3:1.

[3] Reading the parable of the Prodigal Son in its context (Luke 15:1-2) suggests that it is the *elder* brother who represents Jesus' analysis of those to whom the parable was addressed in the first place.

Homesick?

The Welsh have a word for the longing we feel for home, or for the past: *hiraeth*. Homesickness. It is often a distinctive emotion of people who come from small countries or close communities which have their own cultures, language, songs, traditions, and landscape. We can never be fully at home anywhere else.

There is a spiritual *hiraeth* in us all – an unsatisfied longing for communion with God, a sense of being far away from the Father's home. Like the prodigal son in Jesus' parable, however, we often mistake its significance. He seems to have blamed the aches caused by his own self-centredness and his wayward desire for autonomy on the character of his father – who in fact proves to be a generous father indeed!

Here is the real 'projectionism' in our lives! The younger son in Jesus' parable blamed his dissatisfaction on his father rather than seeing it for what it really was – the alienation in his own heart. Jesus' portrayal of him powerfully illustrates the 'projectionism' of sin: we impute to God the disposition we ourselves have towards him. This is an ancient tragedy. It is exactly the warped spirit the serpent in the Garden of Eden encouraged when he suggested to Adam and Eve that God had set them in a garden of plenty and cynically forbidden them to enjoy any of it.[1]

Thus our spiritual homesickness becomes a burden we try to throw off, but never can.

---

[1] Genesis 3:1.

The author of Ecclesiastes speaks about the a *'inyān* that God has given to us. The Hebrew word means something that keeps us busy, or preoccupies us. The NIV translates it as 'burden'.[1] God 'has put eternity into man's heart'.[2]

This is a burden to us, because it means that we can never be satisfied, nor fully experience what we were created to be, without the knowledge of the Eternal Father. As Augustine puts it in the opening section of his *Confessions*, 'You have made us for yourself, and our heart is restless until it rests in you.'[3] We cannot escape it. We can try to silence it; we can run from it; we can suppress it; eventually we may even repress it, and deceive ourselves; but it will not go away.

This must be why militant atheists who profess not to believe God exists often seem to be so angry about him as well as about those who believe in him.

Speaking at a memorial service for his father Sir Kingsley Amis, the novelist Martin Amis unconsciously illustrated this. He recounted a conversation between his father and the Russian author and poet Yevgeni Yevtushenko. Hearing that Sir Kingsley was an atheist, and not a Christian (as he perhaps imagined all British people at the time were), Yevtushenko asked him if it was true that he did not believe in God. Kingsley Amis replied, 'Well, yes. But it's more than that. I hate him!'[4]

---

[1] Ecclesiastes 3:10. This is certainly a more vivid, and perhaps more sensitive, translation than ESV's 'business'.

[2] Ecclesiastes 3:11.

[3] Augustine, *Confessions*, I. i (1). Translated with an Introduction and Notes by Henry Chadwick (Oxford: Oxford University Press, 1991), 3.

[4] Reported by Caroline Davies in *The Telegraph*, October 23, 1996.

The story was told with great effect and to the amusement of the audience. No wonder. The inherent contradiction was indeed amusing, laughable. How could anyone 'hate' a God in whom he did not believe?

But Kingsley Amis was actually giving away the truth about himself. In an unguarded moment he failed to suppress or repress it. The God he denied he nevertheless knew existed and he hated him for it. This is exactly Paul's assessment. Men

> suppress the truth. For what can be known about God is plain to them ... they are without excuse. For although they knew God, they did not honour him as God or give thanks to him, but they became futile in their thinking, and their foolish hearts were darkened. Claiming to be wise, they became fools ...[1]

We cannot cure our homesickness by denying that we suffer from it.

But there is hope for the spiritually homesick: Jesus Christ drank the cup of undiluted *hiraeth* for us, when on the cross he experienced alienation from God.

During the last days of his life Jesus began to sense more than ever that on the cross he would find himself in a 'far country'[2] – exiled not merely from earthly Eden, but from heaven itself. He was taking the place of prodigal sons. In his last hours he experienced a deep distress, a loneliness, a disturbance of his whole being, even a sense of abandonment. He cried out, 'My God, why have you forsaken me?'[3]

[1] Romans 1:19-22.
[2] The expression Jesus uses of the Prodigal Son in Luke 15:13.
[3] Mark 14:33-34; Matthew 27:46.

That was the ultimate *hiraeth*. But he endured it so that we might never need to. It was for this that he was born in Bethlehem. As a greater literary figure than Sir Kingsley Amis once wrote:

> A Child in a foul stable,
> Where the beasts feed and foam;
> Only where he was homeless
> Are you and I at home;
> We have hands that fashion and heads that know,
> But our hearts we lost – how long ago!
> In a place no chart nor ship can show
> Under the sky's dome.[1]

Prince of Peace

It seems to be obligatory at Christmas time for famous 'personalities' to respond to the rather tired, standard question: 'What is your greatest wish for this Christmas?' by saying something like: 'World peace ... if there could just be peace in the Middle East, in Africa; the end of terrorism, an easing of the tensions in the Far East ... that's my deepest Christmas wish this year.'

World peace is a worthy aspiration. But if the nations will not have peace with God they cannot have peace among themselves. The Prince of Peace said so. Quite apart from other considerations there can be no lasting world peace when world leaders seek power for themselves, encourage a nationalism built on the hatred of others, feather their own nests, cheat on and divorce their wives, or stand on the faces of little men. So, while we pray that there may

[1] G. K. Chesterton, 'The House of Christmas'.

CHILD IN THE MANGER

be cessation of hostilities, we do not imagine that this is the same as *peace*. Only false prophets tell us that there is peace when there is no peace.[1] The true prophet exposes our foibles. He urges us not to be so foolish as to think that we genuinely long for world peace when in our individual lives we ignore, reject, or scorn the promise of ultimate peace with God through Christ.

The gospel offers us peace in Christ – an assurance that God's judgment against our sin has been dealt with in him.

This is why the coming child was to be called 'the Prince of Peace'. Isaiah announced him as such early in the first half of his prophecy. But it is only in the second half that he begins to see more clearly what this means. As he peers into the future he sees another figure emerging. God calls him 'My servant'.[2]

The Servant

In the passages where he appears, the Servant speaks only occasionally for himself. But most of the time Isaiah is a by-stander, observing what the Servant of the Lord *does* rather than *says*. He has a special, indeed unique relationship with God. He is the one in whom God's covenant promises are embodied.[3] His whole life is marked by faithfulness expressed in obedience to his Father.[4] Yet despite this he experiences deep suffering.

Isaiah overhears him speak:

[1] Jeremiah 6:14; 8:11.
[2] Isaiah 42:1; 49:6; 50:10; 52:13.
[3] Isaiah 42:6; 49:6. Cf. 2 Corinthians 1:20.
[4] Isaiah 50:4b-5.

> I gave my back to those who strike,
> > and my cheeks to those who pull out the beard;
> I hid not my face
> > from disgrace and spitting.[1]

He is beginning to sound like someone we recognise.

Can it be that *this* is the same person described as Immanuel, Wonderful Counsellor, Mighty God, Everlasting Father, Prince of Peace? Surely not! For as Isaiah strains hard to see this figure, he hears noise and anger, the sound of scourging, and he sees criminals and a rich man's grave. It is deeply unsettling. In the midst of the scene stands the Servant of the Lord. But now he is like a lamb being led to the slaughter. There he stands, silent, like a sheep before its shearers. He has nothing to say. He is being treated as guilty, although he is clearly innocent.[2]

What is happening?

Isaiah begins to see. He sees more clearly now – although the specific identity of the Servant continues to elude him. He strains, but he hears no name, only the words 'My Servant'.[3]

But whoever he is,

> Surely he has borne our griefs
> > and carried our sorrows;
> yet we esteemed him stricken,
> > smitten by God, and afflicted.

How can this be? Why is this? Isaiah is puzzled.

Now, at last, he sees it:

[1] Isaiah 50:6.
[2] Isaiah 52:13 – 53:12 contains the extended description.
[3] Isaiah 52:13; 53:11.

But he was wounded for our transgressions;
> he was crushed for our iniquities;
upon him was the chastisement that brought us
> peace,
> and with his stripes we are healed.
All we like sheep have gone astray;
> we have turned – every one – to his own way;
and the LORD has laid on him
> the iniquity of us all.[1]

Immanuel, the child born of the virgin, will be the Suffering Servant. He will indeed be the Wonderful Counsellor, the Mighty God, the Everlasting Father, and the *Prince of Peace*. As the plot line of the Bible unfolds into the New Testament it becomes clear who this person is. Now we can understand the clues. It is Jesus! He is the one who raises his nail-scarred hands and says, '*Shalom!* I have borne your sins, now I give you my peace.'[2]

In order to do this our Lord went to a realm where Psalm 23 seemed no longer to function. Instead of being able to say, 'Even though I walk through the valley of the shadow of death, I will fear no evil, for you are with me', he went into the dark valley of Calvary to cry, 'My God, why is the 23rd Psalm not working for me here? David said that even when he walked through the valley of the shadow of death you would be with him. But you have forsaken me – why?' The Prince of Peace was chastised to bring us peace.

All of this was still to unfold when Isaiah wrote. But long in advance of the event he detected the *true* meaning

[1] Isaiah 53:4-6.
[2] Luke 24:36.

of Christmas. It involves the birth of Jesus-Immanuel. He is the Wonderful Counsellor who has God's wisdom for us in a world of darkness. He is the Mighty God who has the power to deliver us from our bondage. He is the Everlasting Father who can bring us into God's family. He is the Prince of Peace who came to bear our guilt and comes to bring us his *shalom*.

> **Jesus said:** 'I am the light of the world. Whoever follows me will not walk in darkness, but will have the light of life.' He shows me the way.

> **Jesus said:** 'If the Son sets you free, you will be free indeed.' He delivers me from bondage.

> **Jesus said:** 'I will not leave you as orphans; I will come to you.' He is able to take me home into the family of the Father.

> **Jesus said:** 'Peace I leave with you; my peace I give to you. Not as the world gives do I give to you. Let not your hearts be troubled, neither let them be afraid.'[1] He gives me peace.

Jesus Christ is not only a Rescuer; he is a *complete* Saviour. Everything I lack in my emptiness is found in his fullness and given to me in his grace.

To us

But did you notice *exactly* what Isaiah wrote? '*To us* a child is born, *to us* a son is given.'

Centuries later angelic prophets announced good news to shepherds in the Bethlehem fields: '*To you*, this day,

[1] See John 8:12; 8:36; 14:18; 14:27.

in the city of David, a Saviour is born, Christ the Lord.' Emmanuel is *for us*, just as Jesus was *for* the shepherds. Of course, because Jesus *is* Immanuel!

Is he yours?

Then, if you ever underline verses, or write little notes in the margins in your Bible, do this:

- Look up Isaiah 9:6.

- Underline the words 'to us'.

- Then write in the margin 'to me' –

> *to me* a child is born,
> *to me* a son is given,
> and the government of *my life*
>   will be on his shoulders

because

> He is *my* Wonderful Counsellor,
> He is *my* Mighty God,
> He is *my* Prince of Peace,
> He is *my* Everlasting Father.

Jesus was born to be all of this for us.

But first he was born of a teenage girl in a small country in the Ancient Near East.

To that part of the story we now turn our attention.

6

The Burden

'Equality' is one of the big words of our time. Equal rights, equal opportunity, equal remuneration, and of course equality of the sexes. 'Equality and justice for all' is the slogan of our day as activists and politicians clamour for 'A fair and equal society'.

God created equality in the beginning, according to the Bible's opening chapter. It tells us that there is absolute equality in our basic defining characteristic as human beings. We have been made as the image of God, both male and female.

But also in its opening chapters the Bible underlines that *equality* is not the same thing as *identity*. There are some things a woman can do that a man cannot! The most obvious? She can give birth to a child. She can look at another human being and think, 'You once lived inside my body and depended on me. I carried you as a burden within me for nine months; I agonised to bring you to birth; you fed from my body.'

A mother has a unique relationship to the child she bore. Fathers can love their children; adopting parents can say, 'We *chose you* as our son or daughter.' But only a birth mother can say, 'You were once a life lived within me.' So when a woman is told, 'You are going to have a baby', her entire life changes. She will always be the mother of the person who once lived within her.

In the United Kingdom a woman is on average about twenty-eight years old before she hears the life-changing words, 'You are going to have a baby!' But two thousand years ago in Nazareth, an unprepossessing town in Galilee, somewhat despised by those who did not call it 'home',[1] a young woman nearer half that age heard those words.

The reason we know so much about this girl's experience was not that she was so young when her whole world was changed. It was that her baby would change the world.

But she did not hear the words from her family doctor or her gynaecologist. She heard them from an angel whose name was Gabriel.

The teenage girl's name, of course, was Mary. This is her story. It is just possible that, as an elderly woman, she told it to Luke as he was researching the materials for his Gospel. It is easy to hear Mary's voice in Luke's narrative.

The story[2]

My name is Mary.

I was brought up and lived in Nazareth in Galilee.

I was betrothed to a man called Joseph. He came from

---

[1] See John 1:46.
[2] The narrative is recorded in the third person in Luke 1:26-39.

the David family line. In Jewish law we were technically married, but our wedding day was still to come and so I was still at home – and a virgin.

I did not know that one of my relatives, Elizabeth, was going to have a baby. Her husband Zechariah had been told by an angel that their prayers had been answered (they were 'getting on' a bit!). But then about six months later the angel – he told me his name was Gabriel – visited me too.

He came into the house and said:

'*Shalom*! The Lord's grace is on you – he is with you!'

I was stunned. My mind was racing – what did this mean? But then he said to me:

'There is no need to be afraid, Mary, for God has engraced you. Listen: you are going to conceive and have a son. You must give him the name "Jesus". He is going to be great and will be called the Son of the Most High. And the Lord God will give him the throne of his father David, and he will reign over the house of Jacob forever, and of his kingdom there will be no end.'

I asked the angel immediately, 'How will this happen? I am a virgin.'

His reply was as follows:

'The Holy Spirit will come upon you, and the power of the Most High will overshadow you; therefore the child to be born will be called holy – the Son of God. And, Mary, you are not the only one who is going to have a baby! Your cousin Elizabeth – yes, even at her age – has also conceived a son. She is already six months pregnant, even though she has not been able to conceive in all these years! Remember, nothing will be impossible with God.'

All I could think to say was, 'I am the servant of the Lord; let it be to me according to your word.'

And then he left.

I thought there was only one thing I should do – so I went to spend the next couple of months or so with Elizabeth in the Highlands.

We are told only the most basic details. We have no idea what she told her parents, or whether they agreed that this was the best thing to do. There is no suggestion that she spoke to Joseph. In fact the impression we have in Matthew's account (which we will see focuses on Joseph's side of the story) seems to suggest that he heard at second hand that Mary was expecting a child.[1]

Mary

Apart from Gabriel's description of Mary we know relatively little about her. We can however take some educated guesses from the hints the Gospels give us.

When we first meet Mary in the Gospels she was probably around thirteen or fourteen years old. That was the customary age for betrothal and marriage in her culture. It seems fairly certain that she was brought up in a family of real believers. For one thing, her relatives, Elizabeth and her husband Zechariah, were admired for their faith. Luke describes them in glowing terms:

> They were both righteous before God, walking blamelessly in all the commandments and statutes of the Lord.[2]

[1] Matthew 1:18-25.
[2] Luke 1:6.

This description may not make these two sound particularly attractive to modern ears. But to be 'righteous' does not mean to be 'self-righteous' – if anything it implies the reverse. Nor does 'blameless' mean being 'holier-than-thou'. In the vocabulary of the Bible these were hugely attractive descriptions; Elizabeth and Zechariah were the kind of couple that – with the one exception of their childlessness – you would admire, want to be like, and deeply respect.

Perhaps Mary's parents were like that too. They had, after all, arranged a marriage for her to a man who shared their faith. Joseph was cut from the same cloth as the much-admired Elizabeth and Zechariah. And in case we imagine that would not be much fun for a fourteen-year-old girl, Luke records a few verses later on a poem Mary composed that makes it clear she also loved the Lord. She was soaked in Scripture![1] All in all she was a young woman who knew the grace of God in abundance, and whose life expressed it. And like anyone of whom that is true – since by definition if we have received much grace we know ourselves to have sinned much – she was surprised that the Lord had chosen her for a very special task.

Gabriel carefully explained who the baby would be, and how it was going to be possible for her to be his mother. Although his message is succinct, taking up only three verses in the Gospel, it is tightly packed. It also assumes that Mary had a very good knowledge of the Jewish Bible. There is significance in every phrase:

[1] See Luke 1:46-55. Mary's words contain multiple allusions to passages in the Old Testament.

You will conceive in your womb and bear a son, and you shall call his name Jesus. He will be great and will be called the Son of the Most High. And the Lord God will give to him the throne of his father David, and he will reign over the house of Jacob forever, and of his kingdom there will be no end.[1]

There are so many echoes of Old Testament prophecies in these three verses that an entire Bible quiz could be created on the basis of them!

You will conceive in your womb and bear a son. Mary is first of all addressed in words that clearly echo the promise recorded by Isaiah: 'Behold, the virgin shall conceive and bear a son.'[2]

He will be great. Isaiah had also spoken of the fourfold ministry of the Messiah, including his identity as 'Mighty God' – echoed here in the baby who will be 'great'.[3]

And will be called the Son of the Most High. The words are reminiscent of Daniel's vision of the Son of Man who approaches the Ancient of Days, the Most High, and receives his kingdom and shares the spoils of his victory.[4]

And the Lord God will give to him the throne of his father David. For Mary and her family circle this was one of the great promises about the Messiah enshrined in the pages of the Old Testament.[5] Since both Mary and Joseph

[1] Luke 1:31-33.
[2] Isaiah 7:14.
[3] Isaiah 9:6.
[4] Daniel 7:25, 27.
[5] See 2 Samuel 7:8-17; Jeremiah 30:9; Ezekiel 34:24; 37:24; Hosea 3:5.

belonged to David's family line, this promise involved their wider family circle. But now Mary was being told the promise was not only made to her family in general terms, but would come to fruition through her in particular. Despite the fact that David's line was now reduced to a young peasant girl and her beloved carpenter, it was in their family that the Messiah was to be born. Hadn't God said through Isaiah that when the Promised One came it would be 'as in the day of Midian'? Then he would use the small, the insignificant, the weak, and the poor to be instruments of his triumph. Then it would be clear that the work was God's and not man's (or woman's for that matter).

And he will reign over the house of Jacob forever, and of his kingdom there will be no end. Furthermore this Davidic King's reign would last forever, like that of the promised King in Psalm 72 and the Son of Man in Daniel 7.[1] And he would do so over 'the house of Jacob' – language that was used to refer not only to ethnic Israel but to all those who would come in faith to Jesus Christ.[2]

But there is one more statement in Gabriel's message:

And you shall call his name Jesus. All these other statements tell us about the Old Testament's expectation of who the coming child would be. But as Peter writes, the

[1] Psalm 72:5, 17; Daniel 7:14. This promise was rooted in the original David promise in 2 Samuel 7:13, 16.

[2] Amos 9:11-12. Notice the use of these verses in Acts 15:15-17 where it is clear that the apostles applied the prophecy not along literalistic lines (the rebuilding of physical ruins) but spiritually in terms of the new community God was creating in the church of Christ.

prophets themselves were left wondering 'what person or time the Spirit of Christ in them was indicating when he predicted the sufferings of Christ and the subsequent glories'.[1] Mary was the first person to know the answer. He was to be her baby; and his name was to be 'Jesus'.

So, 'what's in a name?' In the case of Jesus – *our salvation*. 'You shall call his name Jesus', said the angel later, explaining things to Joseph, 'for he will save his people from their sins.'

A name with a history

Several men in the Old Testament had the Hebrew name Jesus (Jeshua, or variants of it). Of these, the most significant was Moses' successor, Joshua the son of Nun. His name means: Yahweh (the covenant name for God) saves.

Joshua's calling from God was to lead his people into the Promised Land, in order to give them 'rest'.[2]

'Rest' is a more significant idea in the Bible than might appear at first sight.

• It was built into God's original creation pattern for us in the gift of the seventh day as a day of rest.[3]

• Noah's parents chose his name because they hoped that 'this one shall bring us relief'.[4] They may well have

[1] 1 Peter 1:11.

[2] See Exodus 33:14; Deuteronomy 3:20; 12:10; 25:19; Joshua 1:13, 15; 14:15; 21:44; 22:4; 23:1.

[3] Genesis 2:1-3.

[4] Genesis 5:29. The name Noah sounds like a Hebrew word for rest and comfort.

been hoping their son would be the seed of Eve who would bring deliverance from the curse.[1]

• Rest was what God promised to his people in the land he planned to give them. Indeed looking back on the Exodus story the prophet Isaiah saw 'rest' as its ultimate goal: 'The Spirit of the LORD gave them rest.'[2]

• Rest was what was promised to David and the kingdom he would establish.[3]

• Rest was what awaited God's people when they returned from exile.[4]

This is why the law God gave to Moses built the concept of rest into the whole fabric of life. Thus weekly Sabbath rest was supplemented by the Sabbath year and then every fifty years by the 'Great Sabbath Year of Jubilee Rest' when slaves were set free and debts were cancelled.[5]

Clearly the essence of the law was a restatement of God's original purpose for life, but now it was

(1) couched in negative language appropriate to sinners and

(2) applied to the life of one nation in a specific land (a situation that was never intended to be a permanent arrangement. It was an interim arrangement until the day when Christ would make the kingdom of God an

[1] Genesis 3:15.
[2] Isaiah 63:14.
[3] 2 Samuel 7:11; 1 Chronicles 22:6-10.
[4] Jeremiah 46:27.
[5] Leviticus 25:1-34.

international family – as began to happen on the Day of Pentecost).

Life in harmony with God's law was a life of *shalom*, peace, well-being, salvation – in a word, *rest* in the Lord.

The Letter to the Hebrews tells us that Joshua the son of Nun did not, and could not, give the people true rest.[1] The entrance into and occupation of the land was only a picture of the reality which would be accomplished through Joshua-Jesus the son of Mary. A greater exodus was needed for true and lasting spiritual rest. This is the exodus that Jesus accomplished at Calvary, which was the theme of his conversation with Moses and Elijah on the Mount of Transfiguration.[2]

This background enables us to hear more clearly the significance of Jesus' famous words:

> Come to me, all who labour and are heavy laden, and I will give you *rest*. Take my yoke upon you, and learn from me, for I am gentle and lowly in heart, and you will find *rest* for your souls. For my yoke is easy, and my burden is light.[3]

Because he can keep this promise he is called 'Jesus, Saviour'.

---

[1] Hebrews 4:8.

[2] Luke tells us that when Moses and Elijah appeared in glory on the Mountain they spoke with Jesus about his 'departure [literally his *exodus*] which he was to accomplish at Jerusalem' (Luke 9:30-31). His 'hour' was the hour of the true 'exodus'.

[3] Matthew 11:28-30.

How?

But the announcement of the baby's identity left Mary with a question: 'How will this be, since I am a virgin?'

She is not asking the question with the same scepticism that had marked Zechariah when he was informed that Elizabeth was going to have a child. 'How shall I know this?' he had asked. Gabriel rebuked him for his unbelief and struck him dumb for a season! No, Mary believes it will indeed happen as the angel has said. But how? After all, she is a virgin. Does Gabriel mean that perhaps a year or so after her wedding day she and Joseph will rejoice in having their own son? But Mary must have sensed that could hardly be what he meant – given the exalted language in which he had described the son who would be born! But how would he come?

Gabriel's stunning answer was that Mary would still be a virgin when her son was conceived.[1]

The Spirit's ministry

We usually speak about the Virgin Birth, and indeed rightly so. Matthew underlines this by saying that Joseph 'knew her not until she had given birth to a son'.[2] But Jesus' birth was not supernatural. It was a normal delivery. Mary must have gone through all the ordinary pains and struggles of a birthing mother. While some Christians have held the view that Jesus' birth would have been 'painless' there is nothing in the text of the New Testament to support or suggest this – and indeed everything points against it. Not only so, but

[1] Luke 1:35.
[2] Matthew 1:25.

his birth – as is always true, but was especially true in the first century – was a dangerous time. Infant and maternal mortality in childbirth was high by comparison with such rates today. The coming of the Son of God did not bypass the pains of birth for mother or for child.

The Virgin *Birth* was therefore a confirmation of the more fundamental event that lay behind it – the Virgin *Conception*. While Jesus' birth was 'natural' his conception was 'supernatural'. It was important that both Mary and Joseph knew that. She was told:

> The Holy Spirit will come upon you, and the power of the Most High will overshadow you; therefore the child to be born will be called holy – the Son of God.[1]

Joseph was told:

> Do not fear to take Mary as your wife, for that which is conceived in her is from the Holy Spirit.[2]

So these twin events – the Virgin Conception and the Virgin Birth – belong to the basic substance of the Christian faith. They are part and parcel of the most commonly used confession of faith in the Christian church, 'The Apostles' Creed':

> I believe in God the Father Almighty ...
> And in Jesus Christ his only Son, our Lord,
>   who was conceived by the Holy Ghost,
>   born of the Virgin Mary ...

The Christian doctrine of the Virgin Birth continues to raise a whole host of questions which would require a

[1] Luke 1:35.
[2] Matthew 1:20.

book-length study to answer.[1] One of the most frequently asked is: 'Do I need to believe in the Virgin Birth of Jesus in order to be a Christian?'

A Christian without believing in the Virgin Birth?

It seems an obvious question to ask. But often when people ask this as their first question about the Virgin Birth they are putting the cart before the horse. Their focus is on Mary: how could she give birth to a child if she was a virgin? What we do not usually realise is that this approach is a little like using a microscope rather than a telescope to see the moon. It is not because of any special feature in Mary that there is a Virgin Birth, but because of what is unique about the identity of her child. Look at the event in the light of who *he* is and we soon discover that the picture becomes much clearer.

Several features of the Gospel narrative are worth remembering in this context.

1. The two Gospel narratives that record the events surrounding Jesus' birth – written by Matthew and Luke – unfold in different ways, but both focus on the Virgin Birth.

Matthew tells us about Joseph, a star, wise men, and King Herod. Luke tells us about Mary and shepherds and angels. The same event is described from two different perspectives in the context of Gospels that tell us different but complementary things about Jesus.

---

[1] The classic work on the subject is still J. Gresham Machen, *The Virgin Birth* (New York: Harper, 1930).

Nevertheless there are three features that anchor both accounts:

- Jesus was born in Bethlehem.

- Mary was his mother and she was married to Joseph.

- Mary was still a virgin when he was born.

Since Mark and John make no reference to it there was no need for these two authors to make this up. Nor were they naïve writers ('the kind of people who believe in a virgin birth'). Luke, after all, was a physician.

2. The conception of Jesus in the womb of Mary was a *supernatural* event, a miracle.

Partly because of a faulty mechanistic world-view we have a tendency to pigeon-hole 'natural' and 'supernatural' events. Natural events we think take place basically under their own steam; supernatural events involve unusual and spasmodic divine interventions.

Scripture however teaches us that *everything* that takes place does so because of the sovereign (and therefore *supernatural*) activity of God. Your birth, my birth, did not take place apart from his providential upholding, sustaining, governing, and directing hand!

So we need to have a much clearer understanding of biblical teaching than is often the case. Otherwise we will assume we are living in a largely non-supernatural world in which God only occasionally intervenes. In fact we are living in a world that continues to exist only because of ongoing supernatural activity. While we sometimes think in terms of God filling in the occasional gaps where nature does not seem to work in its usual way, Scripture teaches us that he is actively engaged in everything that happens. As John Donne observed, if everything that happens took place only once we would be tempted to say 'That's a miracle!'

Since this is how Scripture views our world it understands that while the Virgin Conception is a unique act of God it is not an example of God 'interfering' with nature whereas most of the time he takes a 'hands-off' approach. No, miracles are not so much events in which God acts *against* nature, but unusual actions he takes *within* nature in order to save or preserve it.[1]

3. According to Scripture the birth of Jesus was not the first time someone truly and fully human was created in a special way by God.

There are, of course, unexpected births recorded in the Bible. Elizabeth's son John the Baptist was one – conceived when everyone assumed his parents would not be able to have children. But there are also special acts of creation. Think back to the beginning. Genesis tells us that Adam was created out of the dust. Eve was created out of Adam.[2]

Scripture teaches us that God is Creator of the heavens and the earth who brought them into being *ex nihilo*, out of nothing. He also created our first parents from already existing material yet without human agency. Believe this and we are driven to echo Gabriel's words to Mary: 'For nothing will be impossible with God.'[3]

---

[1] In very technical terms miracles are not *contra naturam* (against nature) so much as *contra peccatum* (against sin and what it has done to nature).

[2] Genesis 2:7, 22.

[3] Luke 1:37.

So the Virgin Conception was a unique event. But it was preceded by God speaking a world into being from nothing, and bringing a man into being from dust, a woman from a man, and then another man from a woman. It would be followed by the resurrection of a man who was crucified, dead, and buried.

Thus Scripture sees the conception of Jesus as unique. But it does not view it outside of the context of other ways in which God has shown the greatness of his power.

Given this biblical teaching, then, there is a deep-seated coherence between the Virgin Conception and the character of God. It might be contrary to expectation but it is not contrary to divine power.

So, is it essential to believe in the Virgin Conception and Virgin Birth in order to be a Christian? Benjamin B. Warfield, the greatest conservative theologian in the early twentieth century, once wrote that the question is actually 'thoroughly impertinent'![1]

There is an obvious reason for this. If you were a Christian living in Cappadocia around say A.D. 40 you would not have read any of the books of the New Testament. Your knowledge of the gospel would be limited to what you had heard. Could you be a real Christian? Of course you could. There is no specific mention of the Virgin Birth in the sermons of the apostles recorded in the New Testament. In this sense it is obviously possible to believe in Jesus Christ as your Saviour and Lord without knowing

[1] B. B. Warfield, 'The Supernatural Birth of Jesus', *The American Journal of Theology*, x, 1906, 21-30; reprinted in *The Works of Benjamin B. Warfield* (New York: Oxford University Press), 1929, vol. III, *Christology and Criticism*, 457.

exactly *how* he came into the world. Judging by Peter's sermon on the Day of Pentecost and Paul's preaching in Athens, many did trust in him without first knowing how he had been born.

The more pressing question needs to be expressed in a different way. 'Is it possible to know the New Testament's testimony to the Virgin Conception specifically and actually deny it, and continue to claim to be a Christian?'

This question is often asked theoretically, not existentially – raised as a form of intellectual self-defence by those who have no intention of becoming Christians in the first place.

Why not believe?

If the question is asked seriously, it should first be met with a series of other questions:

• Why would you not believe it, since it is taught in the only contemporary testimonies we have to Jesus Christ, and the rejection of it places much more than this single doctrine in jeopardy? It is implicit in the rejection of the testimony of the New Testament at this point that the reliability of other parts of it is immediately placed in doubt. Being a Christian then would in a sense involve making up your own 'believable' creed by cobbling together the parts of the New Testament you felt you could reasonably accept. That, far from being authentic Christian faith, is more like post-modernism – create your own Christianity.

• Why would you not believe it, if it is true that all things are possible to God? Doesn't that say something about what you believe – or rather *do not* believe – about him? Expressed differently: if there is any 'supernatural' element in the Gospel record that you do believe, why doubt this one that is so foundational to it?

• Why would you not believe it, since the apostles teach us that Christ's life both begins and 'ends' with a supernatural work of God that has no real parallel? It would, surely, be intellectually inconsistent to believe the New Testament's testimony to the *resurrection* while denying its testimony to the *incarnation*. And, at least according to Paul, if Christ was not raised from the dead and we continue to call ourselves Christians, then we are of all men most to be pitied.

In this light, then, the Virgin Conception and Birth are simply part and parcel of the supernatural character of the Christian faith. They make sense within the context of the power and the purposes of God.

Of course sometimes people say thoughtless and inconsistent things – and even intellectually arrogant and foolish things. But consciously, persistently to deny the Virgin Conception and Birth eventually makes it psychologically impossible with any intellectual *consistency* to trust the teaching of God's word. If the incarnation is an intellectual stumbling block for me, then it follows that the resurrection should be as well, and the ascension, and the second coming, and the reliability of prophecies, and the integrity of the authors of Scripture. Indeed we can go so far as to say: deny the cardinal events of the Virgin Conception and Birth and we have weakened the credibility of the Bible's testimony to Jesus' ministry in its entirety.[1]

Why?

Yet this still leaves a genuine question of faith unanswered: Why?

It is sometimes suggested that true faith never asks 'Why?' In fact it always does so – but in a spirit of *submission* rather than one of unbelief.

The watchwords of two great theologians help us here: 'Believe in order that you may understand' (*Crede ut intelligas*, Augustine of Hippo), so that 'faith is always seeking understanding' (*fides quaerens intellectum*, Anselm of Canterbury). Faith is not produced by unaided human reason. But the gospel we believe is filled with both *truth* that we need to grasp and *divine logic* that we need to follow. It is, therefore, wholly appropriate for us to probe its significance. This is as true of the Virgin Birth as of every other article of Christian faith.

Here then are some of the elements in the inner logic of the Virgin Birth:

(1) Think of young Mary and her husband Joseph. They are to be the parents of Jesus, his guardians, and also his teachers. As those most intimately involved with him they both need to be absolutely certain that Jesus is not merely their son. The Virgin Conception and Birth guaranteed to them – and through them to us – that Jesus is in fact the very Son of God, as Gabriel had promised.

[1] This is not to say that people are always consistent in their thinking, but that they can be illogically inconsistent.

(2) Two related hints given to us by Luke further help us to understand what God is doing.

(i) Gabriel's message to Mary informed her that the Holy Spirit would 'come upon' her and 'overshadow' her.[1] As a result the child she bore would 'be called ... the Son of God'.

Here Luke uses the verb *episkiazō*. In the Septuagint, the Greek translation of the Old Testament with which Luke was very familiar, this same verb was used in Genesis 1:2 to describe the work of the Spirit in the original creation, bringing order and fullness out of 'the earth [that] was formless and void'. The connection is not difficult to see. What God is doing in Jesus is nothing less than beginning a new humanity – but now he is doing so out of the disorder of the old.

(ii) Later on, in his genealogy of Jesus, Luke views Adam as the (created) son of God.[2] He traces Jesus' genealogy all the way back to him to suggest that God is beginning again. But this time he does so by sending his Son to enter the bloodstream of a fallen humanity in order to create a new humanity, what Paul calls the 'new creation'.[3] His first created son Adam fell and brought his entire family into ruin. Now he is starting anew with his Son, but doing so from within the very humanity that has fallen.[4]

---

[1] Luke 1:35.

[2] Luke 3:38.

[3] 2 Corinthians 5:17.

[4] It is surely of interest here that Luke spent so much time with Paul who expresses this concept in the tight logic of Romans 5:12-21 and 1 Corinthians 15:21-28, as well as implying it elsewhere.

(3) A further consideration here is this obvious one. What manner of entry into our world would have been more appropriate for God's Son?

Sometimes theologians who believe in the Virgin Conception suggest that it was not the only way in which Christ could have come.[1] But they do not seem to offer viable alternatives (indeed sometimes they do not offer any alternatives!). Any argument that Jesus could have been the natural child of Mary and Joseph and also the Son of God would seem logically to imply that the incarnation is an amalgam of two persons united together rather than one person possessing two natures. But what lies on the surface of the account of Jesus in the Gospels is that while he is conscious of both his divine identity and his real humanity, he possesses only one 'I'. He is one person.

(4) A final point worth making is this. The Virgin Conception of Jesus *as Saviour* carries with it a significant

---

[1] For a contemporary discussion see *e.g.* Wayne Grudem, *Systematic Theology* (Grand Rapids: Zondervan, 1994), 530: 'On the other hand, it probably would have been possible for God to have Jesus come into the world with two human parents, both a father and a mother, and with his full divine nature miraculously united to his human nature at some point early in his life. But then it would have been hard for us to understand how Jesus was fully God, since his origin was like ours in every way.' The problem with this, of course, is that it virtually requires that the incarnate Christ be *two distinct persons*, since both the human person 'Jesus' and the divine person 'the Son of God' exist separately before the union. This would be reminiscent of the ancient deviation known as Nestorianism after the fifth-century monk and patriarch of Constantinople, Nestorius. This teaching held that in the God-man there are two distinct persons, one divine and the other human. Nestorius was condemned at the Synod of Ephesus in A.D. 431. It continues to be debated whether Nestorius himself really was a Nestorian.

emphasis that is characteristic of the whole Bible's view of salvation: we cannot save ourselves; and none of us can save anyone else. And yet our natural human orthodoxy is *autosoteric* – believing we can save ourselves. The means range from our own good works, to liturgical practices, to self-forgiveness, to self-punishment, and even – perhaps the most popular view of how we qualify for heaven – justification by death (people get to heaven, if not actually become angels, simply because they have died, despite apparently having shown no interest in, or love for, the God of heaven while they were alive).

By contrast the gospel tells us that we are dead now in our sins, and we can do nothing to save ourselves or contribute to our salvation. What the Virgin Conception and Birth demonstrate is that God sets man to one side. He takes hold of our humanity in Mary's womb. Neither she nor Joseph actively contributed to the sovereign work of grace that God began in her womb. All Mary said was 'Let it be to me according to your word.'[1] As Jonah said once, famously, 'Salvation belongs to the LORD!'[2]

Back to Mary

But before we close this chapter we should return to Mary. As she looked back on the dramatic events that transpired in this momentous year in her life, 'Mary treasured up all these things, pondering them in her heart.'[3] She knew the identity of her son. Over the next three decades she must

---

[1] Luke 1:38.
[2] Jonah 2:9.
[3] Luke 2:19.

have come to know Jesus better than anyone – mothers usually do. Then for three years he stepped onto the public stage. At first followed by huge crowds, and then ultimately rejected, betrayed, and denied, he became a victim of perverted religion and failed justice.

Some thirty-four years after Gabriel's visit Mary's son was executed by crucifixion. She herself stood near the cross, helplessly watching the Son whose human nature for the first nine months of his life had been dependent on her, and whom she had lovingly nourished from her own body. In an act of unspeakable tenderness and poignancy the Son committed her into the care of John.[1]

Mary's heart must have broken. Yet she had long known that such a day was coming. When she and Joseph had taken the infant Jesus to the temple to take part in a purification ritual[2] and to present him to the Lord, an aged man had approached them. His name was Simeon. Somehow he had received an intimation through the Holy Spirit that he would live to see the Messiah. The same Spirit providentially led him into the temple just at the time the young couple were there. Mary and Joseph allowed him to hold Jesus. He blessed God; then he blessed them – and added these strange words of prophecy to Mary:

> Behold, this child is appointed for the fall and rising of many in Israel, and for a sign that is opposed (and a sword will pierce through your own soul also).[3]

[1] John 19:26-27.
[2] See Leviticus 12:1-8.
[3] Luke 2:35.

CHILD IN THE MANGER

Thirty-three years later, at Golgotha, the point of the sword ran through her.

That same day, so long before, the Lord brought someone else into the temple to meet Mary – a deeply spiritual woman called Anna. She had known the loneliness of widowhood for many years. Perhaps she was just the comfort and reassurance Mary needed.[1]

But all this still lay ahead. For the moment, on the day when Gabriel came, Mary simply said, 'I am the servant of the Lord. May his word and will be done!'

We need to learn to pray just like that.

> How silently, how silently,
>   The wondrous gift is given!
> So God imparts to human hearts
>   The blessings of His heaven.
> No ear may hear His coming;
>   But in this world of sin,
> Where meek souls will receive Him, still
>   The dear Christ enters in.
>
> O Holy Child of Bethlehem,
>   Descend to us, we pray;
> Cast out our sin, and enter in;
>   Be born in us today.
> We hear the Christmas angels
>   The great glad tidings tell;
> O come to us, abide with us,
>   Our Lord Immanuel.[2]

---

[1] Luke 2:36-38.

[2] From the hymn by Phillips Brooks (1835–93), 'O little town of Bethlehem'.

Although Isaiah had prophesied that the virgin would call her son's name Immanuel, Mary was told to call him 'Jesus', and did so.[1] In one sense 'Immanuel' – God with us – could be a terrifying thought. Perhaps Mary could have sung, with Isaac Watts:

> Till God in human flesh I see,
>   My thoughts no comfort find;
> The holy, just, and sacred Three
>   Are terrors to my mind.
>
> But if Immanuel's face appear,
>   My hope, my joy begins;
> His name forbids my slavish fear,
>   His grace removes my sins.[2]

Now the angel was telling her that Immanuel was coming in human flesh – and he did have another name: 'Jesus'. But that is the theme of our next chapter.

---

[1] Luke 1:31; 2:21.
[2] Isaac Watts, from the hymn 'Dearest of all the names above'.

7

Naming the Baby

It happens on an hourly basis in every country in the world. In fact it takes place as often as 250 times every minute. It is, of course, the birth of a baby.

Whether the parents are rich or poor, wise or simple, eastern or western, northern or southern, there is one decision that must be made. In the Western world it is illegal not to make it!

The baby needs to have a name. It is usually the first thing we enquire about after asking 'Are both well?' It outweighs virtually every other decision. It will mark a son or a daughter for life. For the rest of their days they will react to this one word (or perhaps two). From one point of view it may seem trivial – how important are a few letters from the alphabet after all? Yet it is the big question: *What name?*

For some the choice is straightforward. For others the question of baby's name is simply a catalyst for a whole series of questions. Is there a name we like? Does anyone else have it? What does it mean? Do we need to use a family name? Is there somebody else who has this name who would encourage us to use it – or for that matter discourage us from using it? How will people react to our choice? And then the imponderable question: Will the name suit the child when he or she grows up?

Choosing the name for the baby Jesus turned out to be very straightforward. It was the only thing about his birth that was.

But we are running ahead of ourselves. First there needs to be a pregnancy:

> Now the birth of Jesus Christ took place in this way. When his mother Mary had been betrothed to Joseph, before they came together she was found to be with child from the Holy Spirit. And her husband Joseph, being a just man and unwilling to put her to shame, resolved to divorce her quietly. But as he considered these things, behold, an angel of the Lord appeared to him in a dream, saying, 'Joseph, son of David, do not fear to take Mary as your wife, for that which is conceived in her is from the Holy Spirit. She will bear a son, and you shall call his name Jesus, for he will save his people from their sins.' All this took place to fulfil what the Lord had spoken by the prophet:
>
> > 'Behold, the virgin shall conceive and bear a son, and they shall call his name Immanuel' (which means, God with us).
>
> When Joseph woke from sleep, he did as the angel of the Lord commanded him: he took his wife, but knew her not until she had given birth to a son. And he called his name Jesus.[1]

[1] Matthew 1:18-25.

The chosen name

Joseph found himself in a crisis. He had just learned that Mary, his betrothed, was expecting a child. Matthew's Gospel leaves us with the impression that he heard the news second hand. The only thing of which he was absolutely certain was that he was not the father. It must have been with a heavy heart that he drew the logical conclusion.

He was mistaken. Thankfully he experienced a divine intervention: 'But as he considered these things, behold, an angel of the Lord appeared to him in a dream.' He learned then that behind the conception of Mary's child was the supernatural work of the Spirit of God.

Joseph was also told what the baby's name was to be: 'Mary will bear a son, and you shall call his name Jesus.' In addition, he was given an explanation for the choice: 'for he will save his people from their sins'.[1] From the very beginning of his life, indeed from long beforehand, this child had a divinely given destiny. It was matched by his divinely given name: Yahweh (the LORD) saves.

Most of us discover at some point in our lives why our parents gave us our name. In later years, no doubt, that conversation also took place in the home of the Nazareth carpenter. Perhaps as they paused from work on an oxen yoke one day, Joseph took the opportunity to explain to Jesus what had happened. He needed to know that his name was not the choice of his parents.[2] God had chosen

---

[1] Matthew 1:21.

[2] Two comments should perhaps be made here. (1) Sometimes Christians assume that Jesus simply knew everything – including the story of his conception and birth – because he was God. The New Testament however suggests to us that in his human nature Jesus

it for him because he was God's chosen one. And God had planned his destiny – 'call him Jesus because he will save his people from their sins'. That God had planned his destiny in advance becomes clear from the very beginning: in the first two chapters of his Gospel Matthew mentions five occasions when Jesus fulfilled Old Testament prophecies when he was too young to have had any choice in the matter.[1]

Timetable

As Jesus grew he became increasingly conscious of God's timetable for his life. He referred to the fulfilment of his ministry as a 'time' that had been set out in the divine plan. Hence such comments as, 'My time has not yet come.'[2] Even more precisely he spoke about his 'hour'.[3] In John's Gospel this refers to his passion and crucifixion, which, along with his resurrection, are seen as the foreordained climactic events of his life. He was in a special sense born to die. As Peter would say on the Day of Pentecost:

> This Jesus, delivered up according to the definite plan and foreknowledge of God, you crucified and killed by the hands of lawless men. God raised him up, loosing

had to learn things the same way we do. Orthodox Christianity has always insisted that Jesus' human nature was not invested with unusual powers or knowledge communicated from his divine nature. (2) Then, again, sometimes sensitive consciences object to Joseph being described as Jesus' 'parent'. But he is described this way by the New Testament itself: Luke 2:27, 41. Legally he was – as his act of naming Jesus suggests.

[1] Matthew 1:22-23; 2:5-6; 2:15; 2:17-18; 2:23.
[2] John 7:6, 8.
[3] John 2:4; 7:30; 8:20; 12:23, 27; 13:1; 16:25, 32; 17:1.

the pangs of death, because it was not possible for him to be held by it.[1]

There was a 'definite plan' for Jesus. His life was foreordained for him by his Heavenly Father.

'Foreordination' and 'predestination' are sometimes seen by Christians as controversial terms. Certainly we need to handle them 'with special prudence and care',[2] lest we either misunderstand them or misapply them.

The best brief statement of the biblical teaching was penned by the wise Christian forefathers who wrote the *Westminster Confession of Faith* in the seventeenth century:

> God from all eternity did, by the most wise and holy counsel of his own will, freely and unchangeably ordain whatsoever comes to pass: yet so, as thereby neither is God the author of sin, nor is violence offered to the will of the creatures; nor is the liberty or contingency of second causes taken away, but rather established.[3]

Whenever we find a doctrine to be challenging to us, the most helpful question we can ask is: 'What did Jesus think of this? How did it work out in his life?'

When we ask those questions in connection with God's foreordination and predestination, and search the Scriptures to see how they worked out in Jesus' life, what do we discover?

---

[1] Acts 2:23-24.

[2] *The Westminster Confession of Faith*, III.viii.

[3] *Ibid.* The Scripture references added to the text at this point are: Ephesians 1:11; Romans 11:33; Hebrews 6:17; Romans 9:15, 18; James 1:13, 17; 1 John 1:5; Acts 2:23; Matthew 17:12; Acts 4:27-28; John 19:11; Proverbs 16:33.

There was never a man so conscious that his life had been predestined by God as the Lord Jesus Christ. But this did not turn him into an automaton, or a mere puppet. God's predestination is not biological determinism, nor is it a form of fatalism.

There was, surely, never a freer man, or one more conscious that his actions were his responsibility than our Lord Jesus Christ. He did not become our Saviour by accident on the one hand or merely as a machine on the other. He was destined to be our Saviour; and to that destiny he freely committed himself. He neither saw nor felt any contradiction between God's sovereignty in his life and his own responsibility for his actions. Neither need we.[1]

Naming the baby

There is something else we should notice here. Mary had already been told what her son was to be called.[2] According to Matthew, Joseph was also told that his name would be Jesus. And he adds that Joseph formally 'called his name Jesus'.[3] He took Jesus into his family. In that sense he adopted him as his own, and called him 'The Lord Saves'.

That was an act of faith. We often admire the response of Mary to the announcement that she was going to give birth to the Saviour. She reacted with marvellous faith, as

[1] Frequently in the light of biblical teaching at this point Christians struggle to see how God's sovereignty fits in with the task of evangelism. The brief but classic work by J. I. Packer, *Evangelism and the Sovereignty of God* (London: IVP, 1961) is the best starting place for thinking through these issues.

[2] Luke 1:31.

[3] Matthew 1:25.

the words of the *Magnificat* underline.[1] But God had also done something remarkable in the life of Joseph. In the midst of the deep disturbance of his life he trusted God's word, rested in his sovereign providence, and in a sense he also committed himself to trusting the Saviour. Thus when he names him Jesus, Joseph is saying not only, 'I am taking you as mine, whatever the implications may be', but also, 'I trust that you really are the Saviour God promised to send us.'

Joseph was like one of the Old Testament prophets. He did not know everything we know about the Saviour. But he trusted him on the basis of what he did know.[2]

Perhaps in Joseph's case we can put it this way. His desire was to marry Mary. But here God is saying to him, 'Joseph, you can only have Mary happily if you will have Jesus the Saviour too.'

So, it is very significant that Joseph called him 'Jesus'.

Christians sometimes sing Joachim Neander's hymn 'Praise to the Lord, the Almighty, the King of creation', with its words:

> Hast thou not seen
> How thy heart's wishes have been
> Granted in what he ordaineth?

If ever a man knew this was ultimately true, even with the pain inherent in God's providences, it was Joseph.

---

[1] Luke 1:46-55.
[2] See 1 Peter 1:10-12.

Perfect fit

Jesus' name fitted him perfectly.

Imagine that you were alive perhaps thirty-five years or so after this scene, and you were able to tour Israel. You might meet a man you hear was once blind and ask him, 'How come you are now able to see?' He would reply, 'Because Jesus saved me.'

Then you might meet a deaf man who could now hear perfectly and ask, 'How on earth did you get your hearing back?' The answer would be the same: 'Jesus saved me.'

You could also meet a man who once had been a leper, living in enforced separation from his wife and family, and ask him: 'What happened to you?' Again the same answer: 'Jesus saved me.'

And in the street you might see a man happily walking alongside four of his friends. Someone might say to you, 'Do you see that man over there? He was once paralysed, but now look at the way he is walking!' But as you move towards him the man goes into a house, leaving only his four friends. So you ask them: 'Is it true that your friend was once paralysed? How then is he able to walk today?' And as one their faces would break into wide grins as they responded: 'Jesus saved him. He told him his sins were forgiven and commanded him to walk! Do you want to know the whole story?'[1]

These were only some of the many indications that Jesus proved to be and to do all that the angel had promised: 'he will save his people from their sins'. During his ministry he saved people from the crippling effects of sin.

[1] For these individuals see Mark 10:46-52; 7:32-37; 1:40-45; 2:1-12.

And then, on the cross, he dealt with sin itself – its guilt and shame, its dominion and power. Jesus' name fits him perfectly.

The converted slave trader John Newton knew that:

> How sweet the Name of Jesus sounds
>   In a believer's ear!
> It soothes his sorrows, heals his wounds,
>   And drives away his fear.
>
> It makes the wounded spirit whole,
>   And calms the troubled breast;
> 'Tis manna to the hungry soul,
>   And to the weary, rest.
>
> Dear Name! the rock on which I build,
>   My shield and hiding-place,
> My never-failing treasury filled
>   With boundless stores of grace.
>
> Jesus! My Shepherd, Brother, Friend,
>   My Prophet, Priest and King,
> My Lord, my Life, my Way, my End,
>   Accept the praise I bring.

Perhaps Joseph could have sung that as a quiet lullaby to Jesus.

What name strikes the deepest chord in your heart? The answer may well be the simplest litmus test of where you are spiritually.

Think of the names that are special to you: your mother's name, you father's name, your brother's or sister's name, your wife's or husband's name, your son's or daughter's name, your grandchildren's names. If these names matter to you, they surely matter even more to God. But there is a name that he values above every name – both for himself and for us.

As a young teenager I learned a song that says all this simply and well:

> He did not come to judge the world,
>> He did not come to blame.
> He did not only come to seek,
>> It was to save He came.
> And when we call Him Saviour
>> And when we call Him Saviour,
> And when we call Him Saviour,
>> Then we call Him by His name.

Some Christians – and all who are not – deep down see Jesus as only 'Someone-Come-to-Blame'. It is true: one day he will judge the world. But when he came into the world and was laid in the manger at Bethlehem *he came to save*. That was why he was called Jesus – the Saviour.

Probably very few readers of these pages have never said the name 'Jesus'. But have you ever called him Saviour? Have you ever said something like this to him: 'Lord Jesus Christ, I trust you as my Saviour. You have taken my guilt and shame on your shoulders; your grace and pardon are mine'?

Do you call him by that name?

How much does the name Jesus mean to you? Enough to yield your whole life to him and allow him to transform it?

That – as was discovered by the wise men who found themselves unexpectedly coming to Christ – is what it means to call him Saviour.

8

The First Nowell

Christmas is a time of music and song. Every year around the first week of December (and often even earlier) the canned music in the department stores changes. Familiar Christmas carols and the popular Christmas songs of yesteryear return. (Does anyone really think 'I wish it could be Christmas every day'?)

But however familiar and loved our Christmas music may be, it cannot compare to what a group of shepherds heard on the outskirts of Bethlehem on the night of Jesus' birth.

Their story is told in the Gospel of Luke:

And in the same region there were shepherds out in the field, keeping watch over their flock by night. And an angel of the Lord appeared to them, and the glory of the Lord shone around them, and they were filled with great fear. And the angel said to them, 'Fear not, for behold, I bring you good news of great joy that will be for all the people. For unto you is born this day in the city of David a Saviour, who is Christ the Lord. And this will be a sign for you: you will find a baby wrapped in swaddling cloths and lying in a manger.' And suddenly there was with the angel a multitude of the heavenly host praising God and saying,

'Glory to God in the highest,
　　and on earth peace among those with whom
　　　he is pleased!'

When the angels went away from them into heaven, the shepherds said to one another, 'Let us go over to Bethlehem and see this thing that has happened, which the Lord has made known to us.' And they went with haste and found Mary and Joseph, and the baby lying in a manger. And when they saw it, they made known the saying that had been told them concerning this child. And all who heard it wondered at what the shepherds told them … And the shepherds returned, glorifying and praising God for all they had heard and seen, as it had been told them.[1]

Luke does not make it absolutely clear whether the angels sang. But a multitude of them – an entire army choir of angels – appeared, praising God. Included in their praise was this *Gloria*:

Glory to God in the highest,
　　And on earth peace among those with whom
　　　he is pleased.[2]

These words were not composed for the elite in a great concert hall, but to be heard by the most ordinary of

---

[1] Luke 2:8-20.
[2] Luke 2:14.

people, shepherds watching their sheep in the Bethlehem fields.

According to Jewish tradition it was in this area that the animals for the Jerusalem temple sacrifices were reared. Lambs were used in the morning and evening offerings each day and especially in the Sabbath rituals, as well as on holy days – the first day of the month, at the feasts of Pentecost, Trumpets, and Tabernacles as well as on *Yom Kippur*, the Day of Atonement. And then on Passover itself many thousands of lambs were needed for the pilgrims.[1] In some ways therefore being a shepherd must have seemed a thankless task, in a quite literal sense a 'dead-end job'.

In addition, shepherding seems to have become an occupation sliding down the social scale. Certainly in years following it was not a highly respected one. Shepherds were not regarded with affection and were often assumed to be dishonest. Socially they were among the lowest of the low. So we ought not to romanticise Luke's narrative. His earliest reader Theophilus[2] would have been

[1] See Exodus 29:38-42; Numbers 28:11 – 29:16. Records exist of vast numbers of people being in Jerusalem at Passover time and as many as 250,000 lambs being sacrificed for the Feast. In a fascinating discussion of the numbers that Jerusalem and especially the temple could have held at Passover time, Joachim Jeremias estimated that perhaps 18,000 lambs were sacrificed. Even this figure represents a huge number of animals being driven in from the country for the Feast. Joachim Jeremias, *Jerusalem in the Time of Jesus*, tr. F. H. and C. H. Cave (Philadelphia: Fortress Press, 1969), 77-83.

[2] Luke 1:3. This assumes that 'Theophilus' was an individual and not simply a generic name Luke used to address the reader or hearer of his Gospel ('Theophilus' means 'Lover of God' or 'Loved by God'). The fact that Luke addresses him as 'most excellent' suggests he was an individual of some rank in Roman society.

stunned by angels choosing shepherds as their audience. Certainly none of Luke's educated secular friends would ever have dreamed of beginning a song with the words

> The first Nowell the angels did say
>> Was to certain poor shepherds in fields as they lay.

No – angels should not be speaking to poor shepherds.

Still today in kindergartens or elementary schools, where nativity plays have not yet been replaced by musicals, the annual ritual of choosing children for parts continues. For girls there are usually only two choices: the starring role of Mary, or an also-ran part among the angels. It is a little different for boys. What five-year-old boy really wants to be Joseph and pretend to be the husband of Mary? Better by far to be a wise man – one of only three. And then for the 'also-rans', being a shepherd will have to do.

There is some consolation in being chosen to be a shepherd. You can wrap a blanket over your head, keep yourself to yourself, and become anonymous. The shepherds' parts are almost always for the ordinary types, those who do not have any special talents or personality. If the whole enterprise bores you at age five, the best thing is to be a shepherd!

There is something appropriate in all of this. The angels did not go to Herod or to the wise men with their public announcement of Jesus' birth. The first to hear it were ordinary people, going about their very mundane business; poor men, with no education and few talents, unrecognised, and perhaps rarely trusted. Suddenly in the Bethlehem fields that night angels appeared to them in a blaze of glory.

The announcement was arresting. It also had an interesting shepherd-orientation. They were to go to Bethlehem, the home town of David who became the *shepherd*-king.

Bad news/good news

In fact Luke's account of the nativity of Christ begins with two quite different announcements.

First came *the bad news*. During this whole era Judaea was both subjugated and occupied by the Romans. And now the Roman Emperor, Caesar Augustus, had called for a census, probably in preparation for a new round of taxation, but perhaps also to enable him to enforce an oath of loyalty. That was good news only for tax collectors. It was bad news for everyone else, but especially for the poor. They had to face the inconvenience of travel to their town of origin, where they perhaps still retained a share of some family property. This also meant several days away from earning what was already a subsistence living.[1] And all for what? More taxes. There was plenty to discourage here. The imperial decree brought no comfort or assurance to the poor that they had nothing to fear from Caesar. In fact they had everything to fear.

But then came *the good news* – from an unexpected source, and in the unusual form of a birth announcement. An angel of the Lord brought 'good news of great joy that will be for all the people'.[2] Like all birth announcements

---

[1] For Mary and Joseph this probably meant a round trip of more than a week, especially in light of the fact that Mary was expecting their first child.

[2] Luke 2:10.

this one included the date of birth, the place of birth, and the identity of the baby. Plus there was an unusual twist in the wording:

> Unto you is born this day in the city of David a Saviour, who is Christ the Lord.[1]

To this was added the *Gloria*:

> Glory to God in the highest,
>   And on earth peace among those with whom
>   he is pleased.[2]

The conflict of the ages

The author of a biblical narrative always knows more than the characters involved in it. He is, after all, telling the story from its end point. That is also true here. The shepherds may not have understood the full significance of the angelic message, but Luke, the author of the Gospel, certainly did. He was, after all, a highly educated and sophisticated author, with a considerable knowledge and understanding of the Roman Empire.

The message of the angels stood in stark contrast to the message of the Empire.

After many years of conflict Caesar Augustus was the Emperor who had brought a measure of *peace* to the Empire – the so-called *Pax Romana* or *Pax Augustana*.[3]

---

[1] Luke 2:11.
[2] Luke 2:14.
[3] By no means everyone appreciated the *Pax Romana*. The Roman author Tacitus records (or probably invents) the Caledonian chief Calgacus rousing his troops before the Battle of Mons Graupius with a speech in which he accuses the Romans of devastating lands: 'they

In addition he was hailed as the '*Saviour*'.

One inscription from his reign claimed that 'The birthday of the god has marked the beginning of the *good news for the world*.'

The Emperor Augustus became known as *Imperator Caesar Divi Filius Augustus* – The Emperor Caesar Augustus, *Son of the Divine*.

Luke must have seen the marked contrast in the message from heaven when the true 'Son of the Most High' was born.[1]

Here too there was an announcement of *peace*.

Here too was a *Saviour*.

Here too was *good news for the world*.

Here was the true *Son of the Divine*.

But what a contrast in the character of the Saviour, the nature of the good news, and the kind of peace brought by the gospel.

This sharp contrast simply underlines that what was happening here in Bethlehem was a continuation of the conflict first announced in Eden between the kingdoms of this world and the kingdom of God, between the seed of the serpent and the seed of the woman:

> The LORD God said to the serpent,
> 'Because you have done this …
> I will put enmity between you and the woman,
>   and between your offspring [seed]
>   and her offspring [seed];

---

make a desert and call it peace'. The *Pax Romana* came at a cost to many in the Empire.
  [1] Luke 1:32.

> he shall bruise your head,
>   and you shall bruise his heel.'[1]

At the heart of human history lies this antagonism between the seed of the serpent and the seed of the woman. It manifests itself from Genesis to Revelation, in the opposition between the kingdom of darkness and the kingdom of God, between Babel and the faithful few, between Pharaoh and Moses, between Goliath and David, and between Babylon and Jerusalem, until ultimately reaching its climax in the conflict between the serpent, Satan, and the Son of God who is the seed of the woman.

The announcement from heaven meant that this conflict was now nearing its climax. Two different decrees were being promulgated. One was the decree of Caesar, supposed Son of the Divine, expressing the power and majesty of Rome. It could only bring fear and impoverishment in the present. Soon enough this empire would be one agent in the crucifixion of the seed of the woman. The other, in stark contrast, was the decree of heaven with its good news of the Son of the Most High come to be the Saviour and to bring true peace – purchased at great cost. It was as though God were saying in these events, 'This world always *takes from you*, and ultimately *destroys* you. But there is another world, the one from which these angels come, that *gives to you*, and ultimately *saves* you.'

---

[1] Genesis 3:14-15.

Nothing to fear?

The shepherds' instinctive reaction was fear.[1] But the first words of the angelic visitor assured them: 'You do not need to be afraid.'

There is a great paradox here: they did not need to fear what they most feared! Their reaction to the angelic message is understandable. But it also sets a precedent. Often when people first hear the good news of the gospel they too are afraid of it.

Can it really be true that people *fear* the gospel?

If so it explains a great deal. In the contemporary Western world people often react in deeply hostile ways to even the mention of the name of Jesus. The sheer vigour of the reaction seems to be out of all proportion. What harm has Jesus done them? The response is combative and self-protective. It reveals a deep-down, almost irrational reaction to the gospel – as though there is something to fear. Otherwise, sophisticated people turn into King Herods in their animosity. One might almost think that Christmas itself is only safe for Christians as long as they do not mention Jesus himself!

Nothing seems to have changed in the condition of the human heart. The reaction to Jesus is the same today as it was then: fear which if not quenched will become anger and open hostility. Do people disguise their fear, try to push it away, in order to silence something deep down in their consciences? And does the pressure of the name of Jesus provoke them to open the floodgates of antagonism in desperate self-defence?

[1] The wording of Luke 2:9 is emphatic: 'they feared great fear'.

How right Isaac Watts was:

> Till God in human flesh I see,
>   My thoughts no comfort find;
> The holy, just, and sacred Three
>   Are terrors to my mind.

Another kind of fear

There is, of course, another kind of fear. This was the kind of fear that made Simon Peter occasionally lash out against Jesus. It arises because the gospel that promises eternal life also calls for the sacrifice of our own lives to Christ.

Like many others who took their first steps following Christ as teenagers, I remember the fear of what would happen – fear of what people would say or do. How would my family react when I told them? What would happen at school? Would I lose friends? Part of the good news of the gospel is that nobody ever yields their life to Christ without discovering that he is never their debtor.

These shepherds were not the last ones who needed to hear the message, 'Do not fear.'

> Peter began to say to him, 'See, we have left everything and followed you.' Jesus said, 'Truly, I say to you, there is no one who has left house or brothers or sisters or mother or father or children or lands, for my sake and for the gospel, who will not receive a hundredfold now in this time, houses and brothers and sisters and mothers and children and lands, with persecutions, and in the age to come eternal life.'[1]

[1] Mark 10:28-30.

The announcement

This, then, is the most significant birth announcement of all time. Yet it is marked by a remarkable economy of words. One might almost think that the announcement was paid for by the word! It is so brief. Not a word is wasted:

What? – A birth.

When? – Today.

Where? – In Bethlehem.

Who? – A Saviour, Christ the Lord.

But there is one more essential detail.
Birth announcements in the press tend to have approximately the same form:

On 10th November, in the Craigie Maternity Hospital, to Jane and John Smith, a son, Henry …

But this birth announcement had an unexpected twist. It did *not* read:

Today, in Bethlehem, to Mary and Joseph of Nazareth, a son, Jesus ...

Instead it read: 'To YOU'! '*To you shepherds* this day in the city of David is born a Saviour, who is Christ the Lord.'

This was a dramatically different birth announcement! No mention here of the mother and father. There never was another birth like this infant's birth, just as there never will be another death like the death he will later die. This is a birth (and a death) *for others*. It is for shepherds. It is *for us.* These two words become like punctuation marks in the gospel message.[1]

This is what made the announcement the shepherds heard such good news, such a wonderful gospel. This baby had been born *for them*.

In addition, the angel told them to look for a particular sign.

Sign

In the Old Testament, when God gave his people a fresh promise he also characteristically gave them a sign to reassure them of its reliability.

Of course God's promise can always be trusted. But his reliability is not the issue – ours is. He knows that we are sometimes full of doubts and fears. His signs were visible seals or confirmations of his promise.[2] So when the angel of the Lord gives the word of promise about the birth of the Messiah ('Christ the Lord'), he adds, 'This will be a sign for you …'[3]

Whenever a baby was born in the area where we used to live there were always signs of the event. There might be an artificial stork in front of the house; there were always balloons – blue for a boy, pink for a girl. These signs said 'Rejoice with us! We have a new baby!'

---

[1] For example: Romans 5:8; 8:32, 34; 2 Corinthians 5:21; Galatians 2:20; 3:13. All these statements indicate that the promise of Isaiah 53:4-6 has been fulfilled in Jesus Christ.

[2] This specific language is used of circumcision in Romans 4:11, but it is clear that other covenant signs like the rainbow (Genesis 9:12-17) and the Sabbath (Exodus 31:12-13) functioned in a similar way.

[3] Luke 2:12.

But the sign for this new-born baby was very different.

Of course – he is, after all, 'Christ the Lord', *Christos Kurios*. It would be no surprise in the Roman Empire if a king's birth was marked by some new celestial phenomenon, such as a new star. Wise men would be looking for such things.

But shepherds – what would be a suitable sign for shepherds? They were told that he was the Saviour – what signs would speak most eloquently of this? And what could be the sign that this baby had been 'born *to you*' – shepherds? How would they be able to tell he was a Saviour suited to shepherds and their needs?

> This will be a sign for you: you will find a baby wrapped in swaddling cloths and lying in a manger.[1]

At first it must have seemed puzzling. The Lord lying in a feeding trough, presumably in an outhouse? A Saviour wrapped in swaddling bands?

What did this communicate to these shepherds? They could no more take this in at one hearing than the disciples could later take in the resurrection the first time they heard about it. But what it said was this: 'The Lord has come to redeem the poorest of the poor. You are poor men, and you know what it is for your new-born children to have little. Christ the Lord has come right down to your level. He has come from heaven empty-handed.'

His mother, Mary, had been right:

> He has brought down the mighty from their thrones
> and exalted those of humble estate;

[1] *Ibid.*

he has filled the hungry with good things,
and the rich he has sent empty away.[1]

Bound

The Lord was wrapped in swaddling bands. The one who can 'bind the chains of the Pleiades or loose the cords of Orion'[2] lies now in a manger. His little body, only a few pounds in weight, is firmly bound with cloths because it was feared that otherwise his limbs would be in danger of malformation.[3] The Creator becomes subject to the cultural practices of the first century. The one who populated the forests with trees lies within the bark of one. The one who has always been face to face with his Father now stares into the face of his teenage mother. The one whom the heavens cannot contain is contained within a stable. He who cradles the universe is himself cradled in an animal's feeding trough. Yes, this is the kind of Saviour who is suited to the needs of shepherds! Indeed, if he can save shepherds no one is beyond his ability to save. He has stooped to the lowest of the low in order to raise them up to 'God in the highest'.[4]

Possibly Luke's first readers, living as they did in a culture where observation and a good memory were important, might have remembered the language he used here as they came towards the end of his Gospel. He

[1] Luke 1:52-53.

[2] Job 38:31.

[3] This was the reasoning behind these swaddling bands. The practice continued in many cultures through the nineteenth century but has largely been abandoned. Occasionally it is discussed in the medical literature, but current opinion appears not to favour it.

[4] Luke 2:14.

echoes it when he tells us that once again the Saviour is to be found wrapped in linen bands and lying on borrowed property. The one who began his life wrapped in swaddling cloths and laid in the animals' manger ends it laid in a rich man's rock-hewn tomb, now wrapped in linen bands for a shroud.[1] The shadow of his death is present already in the description of the details of his birth.

One person who grasped this very clearly was the German composer Johann Sebastian Bach. As his great *Christmas Oratorio* progresses we hear these words sung in the first chorale:

> How shall I fitly meet Thee,
>   And give Thee welcome due?
> The nations long to greet Thee,
>   And I would greet Thee too.
> O Fount of Light, shine brightly
>   Upon my darkened heart,
> That I may serve Thee rightly,
>   And know Thee as Thou art.

These words were familiar to the first hearers of *The Christmas Oratorio*. Written by Johann Crüger and first published in 1653 they were ordinarily sung to a tune composed by Melchior Teschner in 1613. But the first listeners must have realised Bach had done something profoundly moving. The tune is not the familiar one by Teschner but comes from the *Passion Chorale* – the tune wedded to Paul Gerhardt's great Good Friday hymn, 'O sacred head, sore wounded':

[1] Luke 23:53.

O sacred head, sore wounded,
 With grief and shame weighed down!
O Kingly Head, surrounded
 With thorns, Thine only crown . . .

O Lord of life and glory,
 What bliss till now was Thine!
I read the wondrous story;
 I joy to call Thee mine.
Thy grief and bitter passion
 Were all for sinners' gain;
Mine, mine was the transgression,
 But Thine the deadly pain.

What language shall I borrow
 To praise Thee, heavenly Friend,
For this Thy dying sorrow,
 Thy pity without end?
O make me Thine for ever,
 And, should I fainting be,
Lord, let me never, never,
 Outlive my love to Thee.[1]

The same melody reappears in the final chorale of *The Christmas Oratorio*, but this time celebrating Christ's triumph.

Bach grasped the heart of the Christmas message: the baby bound in swaddling bands and lying in a wooden manger is destined to be bound again in later life and laid upon wood on the cross of Calvary. He is 'born to save the

---

[1] The hymn is originally from the Middle Ages and was translated by Gerhardt. The English version quoted here was translated from Gerhardt by J. W. Alexander (1804–59).

sons of men',[1] born to die. He has not come for his own sake, nor merely to give joy to Mary and Joseph. He has been born for people such as the shepherds in the fields – 'born *to you* … a Saviour, Christ the Lord', proclaimed the angel.

The shepherds could not have understood all this immediately. All they knew was that the baby had been born for them too.

Yet perhaps these simple shepherds did have some sense of what this message implied. Otherwise why would they have returned to their sheep doing exactly what the angels had done, namely 'glorifying and praising God'? More than that, they rejoiced in 'all that they had *heard* and *seen*'.[2]

Theological field group

Shepherds understood one thing: sheep. But what were these sheep for? Sacrifice. The majority of the lambs birthed in lambing season would die at Passover, the memorial sign to God's people of the night in which the death of a lamb had saved their first-born sons from the judgment of the Angel of Death.[3]

It is not difficult to imagine that these shepherds may on occasion have passed a long night by the fire arguing about religion. No doubt some of them had been brought up as synagogue-goers, perhaps even by faithful parents. Some of them were probably jaundiced by the conviction that religious people were hypocrites.

[1] From Charles Wesley's hymn, 'Hark! the herald angels sing'.
[2] Luke 2:20.
[3] Exodus 12:1-28.

Was there ever a conversation like this?

Jacob: This whole thing is a waste of time! We see these lambs birthed – and for what? Temple sacrifices – supposedly for our sins! Lambs for Passover! How could a lamb substitute for a first-born son? There's no comparison between a lamb and a son! And what good do they do us, sacrificed for our sins? How can a lamb take the place of a human being? Isn't that obvious?

Amos: But what do you think of that promise of Isaiah about the Servant?

Jacob: What do you mean – promise?

Amos: Don't you remember that passage we had to learn at synagogue school, Jacob? I can still recite the whole thing. It's the one that says:

> He was oppressed, and he was afflicted,
>   yet he opened not his mouth;
> *like a lamb that is led to the slaughter …*
>   so he opened not his mouth …[1]

Doesn't it go on to say this?

> But he was wounded for our transgressions;
>   he was crushed for our iniquities;
> upon him was the chastisement that brought us peace,
>   and with his stripes we are healed.
> *All we like sheep have gone astray;*
>   *we have turned every one to his own way;*
> *and the LORD has laid on him the iniquity of us all.*[2]

[1] Isaiah 53:7.
[2] Isaiah 53:5-6.

That's shepherd-talk that, don't you think? It's saying we're like these stupid sheep that keep wandering off. And this Servant – whoever he is – he's like one of these lambs we see birthed for the temple sacrifices and for the Passover. It's all a picture of the Servant.

Jacob: Even so, it's got nothing to do with the likes of us. Who cares about saving us, Amos? We're Bethlehem shepherds, not Jerusalem Pharisees!

In one sense of course Jacob was right. The sacrificial system of the Old Testament was never meant to be 'the real thing'. A later writer in the New Testament would use the same logic: 'It is impossible for the blood of bulls and goats to take away sins.'[1] Or as Isaac Watts put it:

> Not all the blood of beasts
>   On Jewish altars slain
> Could give the guilty conscience peace
>   Or wash away the stain.

But they did point to someone who could:

> But Christ, the heavenly Lamb,
>   Takes all our sins away;
> A sacrifice of nobler name
>   And richer blood than they.[2]

Could this new-born baby be the Saviour come to make the true sacrifice? Perhaps the Lamb of God who would take away the sins of the world had been born?

---

[1] See the argument used in Hebrews 10:1-12.
[2] From the hymn by Isaac Watts (1674–1748), 'Not all the blood of beasts'.

Luke tells us that this was a night that changed the shepherds' lives. As they made their way back to the fields they were 'glorifying and praising God for all they had heard and seen'.[1] They had heard that he was 'Christ the Lord'. They had been told he was 'a Saviour'. Surely if they returned rejoicing and praising God they must have sensed something special about this child who had been born for them?

Johann Sebastian Bach was capable of expressing this mystery in music of the greatest sophistication. But it can be just as truly, if much less grandly, expressed in simple ways – as in the song quoted in the previous chapter which I learned to sing when still a young teenager:

> He did not come to judge the world,
>   He did not come to blame.
> He did not only come to seek,
>   It was to save He came.
> And when we call Him Saviour,
>   And when we call Him Saviour,
> And when we call Him Saviour,
>   Then we call Him by His name.

It is worth repeating that, tragically, people often feel this is exactly and only what Jesus Christ came to do – judge and blame. That can be true even of those – sometimes *especially* of those – who still attend church and are familiar with the language of the Christian faith. Some have even felt that it is easier to go to his mother Mary for sympathy than to go directly to Jesus himself. But he did not come to condemn the world. Yes, his Spirit convicts us

[1] Luke 2:20.

of our sinfulness – but it is in order that we will seek the forgiveness that Christ offers us in the gospel.[1] For he did not come to blame us, but to save us.

This is indeed good news for all people. These angels and their praise are signs that 'Christ the Lord' has been born for us. These swaddling bands and this manger are signs of his humble coming to be our Saviour, the Lamb of God who will take away the sins of the world. This is indeed the greatest birth of all time. No wonder a *Gloria* was sung by the angels.

Before we leave this scene we should perhaps take a last look at these angels.

Angels

Our Western culture, post-Christian though it is, has retained a fascination with angels. But when we look through the pages of the Bible we discover that God seems to have been sparing in granting them opportunities to become visible. Usually they appear in a company only at events of special significance:

• At creation the morning stars sang together, as the book of Job tells us.[2]

• At the giving of God's covenant and law to Moses on Sinai they were present.[3]

• At the return of Christ in glory they will be in his retine.[4]

[1] John 16:8-11.
[2] Job 38:7.
[3] Deuteronomy 33:2.
[4] 2 Thessalonians 1:7.

But here too, at the birth of Jesus, the angels are given the opportunity to express their wonder at the nativity of their King. Their praise is in the form of (1) a doxology directed towards God and (2) a gospel proclamation directed towards men and women:

(1) Glory to God in the highest.

(2) On earth peace among those with whom he is pleased.[1]

Peace. The philosopher Epictetus, a near-contemporary of Luke, wrote, 'The emperor may give peace from war on land and sea. He is unable to give peace for passion, grief and envy.' The *Pax Augustana* could not touch the heart. But the promise of the angels is that Christ will bring us peace, because he is the Saviour.

So here is good news for all people. The greatest birth of all time; an unexpected sign given to shepherds; a magnificent *Gloria* performed by angels.

Peace to whom?

There is one qualification in the angels' message related to the promise of peace. They announce 'peace among those *with whom he is pleased*'.

These words have often been misunderstood, and sometimes our Bible translations are not particularly helpful. When literally translated their meaning becomes clear enough: 'and on earth peace among men *of his good pleasure*'. The angels are not giving these shepherds a moral

[1] Luke 2:14.

lecture: 'Pull your socks up, shepherds. You need to do better! God is not very pleased with you. You need to try harder! Maybe then you will experience more *shalom*!' No, 'those with whom he is pleased' (an unhappy translation) really means 'those who are recipients of God's gracious favour'.

God is not like a department store Santa Claus asking through his white beard, 'Have you been good this year?' – as though we need to qualify for the Christmas gift. Yet all too often that is how we think of him. No. The God who gave his only Son to be born and die for us in order to replace the guilt and shame of our sin with peace is not a glorified Father Christmas. He is a gracious Saviour. His salvation is not given to me because I have done well. It comes when I have sinned, and know that I have displeased him, and need a Saviour.

This is the message of the angels. It is for all.

But not all who hear the message want to receive it. These shepherds – to whatever degree they understood all this – did receive it. A new note came into their lives, a note of 'glorifying and praising God'.[1] It was coupled with a desire to tell others about Christ, so that 'they made known the saying that had been told them concerning this child'.[2]

It is the same today.

Have you ever prayed, 'Lord, may I be one upon whom your saving favour rests'?

---

[1] Luke 2:20.
[2] Luke 2:17. It is fascinating to notice that the shepherds are now doing exactly what the angels had earlier done for them.

When God awakens us we become willing to travel as far as is necessary to find Christ.

At the first Christmas some men did.

9

The Long Journey

Have you ever heard someone say: 'Christmas grew out of the pagan Roman festival of Saturnalia, and is actually a pagan celebration'?

Did it?

The Saturnalia Festival in honour of Saturn was held on December 17 each year and continued for about a week. Normal life was overturned for a brief season of revelry.

And Christians did begin to celebrate Christmas during the Saturnalia holiday. But to say that Christmas is a pagan celebration is as sensible as saying that a Christian who goes to church on Sunday worships the Sun god!

In fact the celebration of Christmas began as a gospel antidote to Saturnalia. It was a way for Christians to point to a true, good, and lasting reason for celebration – not licence to sin but salvation from it through Jesus who was born to 'save his people from their sins'.[1] They wanted to emphasise that the source of real celebration is found only in Jesus Christ.

[1] Matthew 1:21.

The New Testament does not oblige Christians to celebrate Christmas, or for that matter Easter. But the wisdom of the church throughout the ages suggests that if we do not celebrate the incarnation of Christ deliberately at some point in the year we may be in danger of doing it all too rarely and, perhaps, not at all.

One Saviour, many paths?

Jesus claimed to be the only source of salvation and the only way to the Father.[1] But it is remarkable to observe the different paths along which God leads us to salvation's one source – Jesus. Matthew's Gospel provides an account of the path taken by a group of Magi or wise men, who came from the East in search of the new king they believed had been recently born:

> Now after Jesus was born in Bethlehem of Judea in the days of Herod the king, behold, wise men from the east came to Jerusalem, saying, 'Where is he who has been born king of the Jews? For we saw his star when it rose and have come to worship him.' When Herod the king heard this, he was troubled, and all Jerusalem with him; and assembling all the chief priests and scribes of the people, he inquired of them where the Christ was to be born. They told him, 'In Bethlehem of Judea, for so it is written by the prophet:
>
>> "And you, O Bethlehem, in the land of Judah,
>>   are by no means least among the rulers of Judah;
>>   for from you shall come a ruler
>>   who will shepherd my people Israel."'

[1] John 14:6.

Then Herod summoned the wise men secretly and ascertained from them what time the star had appeared. And he sent them to Bethlehem, saying, 'Go and search diligently for the child, and when you have found him, bring me word, that I too may come and worship him.' After listening to the king, they went on their way. And behold, the star that they had seen when it rose went before them until it came to rest over the place where the child was. When they saw the star, they rejoiced exceedingly with great joy. And going into the house they saw the child with Mary his mother, and they fell down and worshipped him. Then, opening their treasures, they offered him gifts, gold and frankincense and myrrh. And being warned in a dream not to return to Herod, they departed to their own country by another way.[1]

Ever since these Magi made their long journey they have captured the imagination of artists, poets, and musicians. They are the ones who tend to feature on the most expensive Christmas cards! They were clearly – even allowing for the exaggerations of Western art that depicts them travelling across the desert as though dressed for a coronation – several cuts above the social class of the shepherds who had earlier arrived at the manger.

The Magi, like all their pagan contemporaries, believed that cosmic forces and events governed, or at least influenced and were related to, human life and history.

Of course in some senses we still believe this. For example, the syndrome known as SAD is well recognised – some people are much more prone to depression in the dark days of winter than they are in the brighter and warmer days

[1] Matthew 2:1-12.

of summer. Often people who live in cold, dark, northern climes seem to have quite different 'personalities' from those who bask in year-round sunshine! The Magi's world-view extended such inter-relations to a far greater degree. For them physical phenomena, like the sight of a new object in the heavens, held deep significance for life on earth. This was also true on the terrestrial level – these same men might well have examined the entrails of an animal to discover auguries about the future.[1]

Despite all this, Matthew understood that God is well able to fulfil his own designs through the limited under-standing and even intellectual misapprehensions of men and women. Thankfully, he still is.

A new star

The Magi had seen a new 'star'. We need not be side-tracked here into a discussion of the nature of the 'star'. As in all areas of scientific classification, the categories used in antiquity were broader and more basic than ours. For these Magi the sky was dominated by the sun and the moon. Other heavenly bodies simply fitted into the broad category of 'star'.[2] For reasons we will later see, they believed this new

[1] Perhaps the most famous illustration of this in antiquity is related to the assassination of Julius Caesar. In his *Lives of the Twelve Caesars*, his biographer Suetonius describes various warning signs of the event: the finding of a tablet in the tomb of Capys (founder of Capua) fore-telling the death of one of the occupant's descendants at great cost to Italy; a bird flying into the Hall of Pompey pursued and destroyed by other birds. 'Julius Caesar', lxxxi.

[2] In the same way 'leprosy' in antiquity was a general category for a variety of skin disorders as well as the condition known today as 'leprosy'.

star meant that a new Jewish king had been born. Thus they set out on their journey to Judaea.

They arrived late, having lost their way once – with almost disastrous results. Indeed by the time they arrived in Bethlehem the peak of the registration period seems to have passed; they found Mary and her infant son no longer in the stable but in the house.[1] Perhaps the innkeeper had been able to find a space indoors for them after the birth.

Whatever clues the Magi saw in this new star they felt themselves caught up in an event of great significance. When eventually 'they saw the child with Mary his mother … they fell down and worshipped him'.[2] Then they had a dream that filled them with foreboding, but which they took to be a divine warning. As a result, instead of returning to King Herod (to whose palace they had mistakenly gone to find the new-born king), they left the country by a different route and headed home.[3]

Searching

The Magi's Christmas began with a new celestial phenomenon – a star had recently appeared that attracted their attention. They followed its movements across the sky until they eventually reached their destination. But *en route* they had taken a wrong turning.

One of the most fascinating elements in this story is that the Magi lost their way at a crucial point *by assuming they could find their own way!* They returned to the right

[1] Matthew 2:11.
[2] Matthew 2:11.
[3] Matthew 2:12.

way again only when they were pointed by the Scriptures to the place where the king was to be born.

That is just as important a lesson for us to learn as it was for the Magi. If we are ever to understand Christmas we need more than a providential event like a star; we need a book – one particular Book.

Despite the legends and the songs and poems that celebrate them, we know very little about these men, and nothing about them as individuals.

But there are some suggestive clues planted in Matthew's narrative.

First, judging from the gifts they brought with them, they were wealthy, or at least had access to considerable resources. Gold, frankincense, and myrrh have never come cheap.

Second, they were scholarly. They were scientists, men of learning – at least that was how they would have been classified in their own day and indeed probably through to the seventeenth century. We often forget that a scientist like Sir Isaac Newton was profoundly interested in what today would be thought of as very 'unscientific' science. But in distinction from the popular view of 'science' someone like Newton was interested in *scientia* – knowledge – wherever, however, and by whomsoever it might be found.

These Magi belonged to that world. They were interested in the nature of things, and in how the physical world had a bearing on people's lives. They watched the stars and presumably they read great books. In both they sought to find the meaning of world events.

From the East

Where did these men come from on this long journey?

Probably from the area known in antiquity as Persia. Possibly from Babylonia, and perhaps from the city of Babylon itself. In modern-day geography they were from Iraq.

Why suggest Babylon?

Babylon was the city to which Daniel and his friends had been taken after Nebuchadnezzar had besieged and conquered the city of Jerusalem.[1] They had been educated in the schools of the Magi and had graduated with first-class honours – *summa cum laude*. He later became President of the College of Magi and Prime Minister of the province of Babylon.[2]

It was Daniel who had famously interpreted King Nebuchadnezzar's terrifying dream of a stone, cut without human hands, rolling down a hill, gathering pace, destroying all the kingdoms of this world, and eventually filling the whole earth.[3] It was in Babylon that Daniel had seen and recorded his night vision of the Son of Man receiving a kingdom from the Most High, the Ancient of Days.[4] In addition, Daniel knew the ancient oracle of Balaam which, like Daniel's vision, also made reference to 'the Most High':[5]

> … the oracle of the man whose eye is opened,
> the oracle of him who hears the words of God,

[1] Daniel 1:1, 3-7.
[2] See Daniel 2:46-49. The events took place in 605 B.C. onwards.
[3] Daniel 2:31-36.
[4] Daniel 7:9-14.
[5] Daniel 7:18, 22, 25 (twice), 27.

and knows the knowledge of the Most High,
who sees the vision of the Almighty …
I see him, but not now;
  I behold him, but not near;
a star shall come out of Jacob,
  and a sceptre shall rise out of Israel …[1]

Perhaps all this became part of the collected oral tradition of the schools of the Magi. A new kingdom, a new king, and a star – it is easy to see how this might influence scholars who studied ancient texts and sought to interpret heavenly signs. Here was a new star – but who was the new king?

Clearly all this had something to do with the Jewish people. So in all likelihood these men set off for Judaea because they believed they were on the brink of solving an ancient puzzle – one that went back into the reign of Nebuchadnezzar and the days of the foreign Magi. Now they were on their way to find the one who had been born, and, as they would naïvely tell King Herod, they were planning to honour him.

We must not think, however, that this journey was a run-of-the-mill research project. Far from it. There must have been other Magi, perhaps many others, who knew the same ancient traditions, who observed the same new star, but did absolutely nothing about it. Yet God in his providence elevated these particular men's pursuit of truth, and led them to make the necessary arrangements to leave home and to go on this extended journey. Did they remember to discuss their plans with their wives?

[1] Numbers 24:15-17.

Many are called, few chosen

Many saw the signs, but few followed them. It always seems to be that way. Many people know about the message the Bible contains. They experience evidences of God's working in their lives, sometimes through joy, at other times through sorrow. There is a tug at the heart – however vague at first it seems to be. Yet at the end of the day, only some respond and seek Christ. We all have access to the same Book; we all experience the pressure of God upon our lives; but not all search for and find Christ.

But these Magi did. They were prepared to put everything else aside in order to find him. For them it was just as Jesus later said:

> Ask, and it will be given to you;
> > seek, and you will find;
> > knock, and it will be opened to you.
> For everyone who asks receives,
> > and the one who seeks finds,
> > and to the one who knocks it will be opened.[1]

Wrong turning

Eventually the wise men knocked on the door of the house where the child and his parents were.

But before that they had taken a wrong turning. They followed the star, it seems, as far as Judaea itself. But then they assumed they could work out the rest of the journey by themselves. Here they assumed that cosmic signs could give way to simple human logic: new king = royal palace.

---

[1] Matthew 7:7-8.

Thus they went to Jerusalem, and made their way to King Herod's Palace.

But they did not find the new king there. Only the old king.

The experience must have been perplexing, not only because of what they did not find there, but also because of what they did.

They did not find the new king – that was perplexing.

They did find Herod – that proved to be perplexing in a different way.

Herod called his own 'magi' – the chief priests and scribes – men whose area of expertise lay in the ancient literature of the Jewish people. Asked if they knew the location of the promised king's birth they had no difficulty in providing the answer. It was found in a book with which they were very familiar, but which was unknown to the visiting Magi. Here the University of Jerusalem could enjoy some one-upmanship over the University of Babylon! The prophet Micah had written,

> And you, O Bethlehem, in the land of Judah,
>> are by no means least among the rulers of Judah;
> for from you shall come a ruler
>> who will shepherd my people Israel.[1]

It could hardly be clearer. Bethlehem was the place; it was David's city.

But this was what must have perplexed the Magi.

Here they stood in Herod's Palace. They had made considerable personal sacrifices in their quest to find the

---

[1] Matthew 2:6; see Micah 5:2.

new king. But these learned and religious men who had immediate access to information about his birthplace seemed to have no interest in finding him, far less in going to worship him! Did they secretly despise these visitors from the East as men with more zeal than knowledge? Sadly they themselves had knowledge but no zeal. They knew the truth, but not its power.

Yet for all their lack of discernment and zeal, they surely saw through Herod's pious words, 'Go and search diligently for the child, and when you have found him, bring me word, that I too may come and worship him.'[1]

This would be amazing if it were not all too familiar. Here were able people, with access to the Bible, but indifference to what the Bible taught. A small company of pagans coming from the East put them to shame.

In some ways, however, this was simply a 'trailer' for what would follow in the course of the new king's life. It is Matthew who records Jesus' words to the chief priests and the elders: 'Truly, I say to you, the tax collectors and the prostitutes go into the kingdom of heaven before you.'[2]

A different 'wrong turning'

If the mistake of the Magi was to assume they could take the final steps to finding Christ on their own, the mistake of Herod's scholars was that they confused Bible knowledge with real faith. The power of God's word had not really registered in their hearts. Even if the Messiah had been born, they could leave that to one side for the moment, and concentrate on more important matters.

[1] Matthew 1:8.
[2] Matthew 21:31.

The Bible is like a mirror, says James. We look at it and forget what we see.[1] Knowing the Bible is not the same thing as entering the kingdom of God. Herod's theologians illustrate that at the beginning of the Gospel narrative. By its end this spiritual sickness has spread all the way up to the head. Later in Matthew's Gospel we read of some of these men or their successors:

> Then they spit on his face and struck him. And some slapped him, saying, 'Prophesy to us, you Christ! Who is it that struck you?'[2]

What a solemn warning that is! The humility of God left these religious men cold. Humility always does that to the proud and self-sufficient. They are not drawn to humble places, or humble babies, far less a humble Saviour.

Yet all this is in keeping with the character of God and the patterns of his working. He humbles the proud and exalts the humble. It is so deliberately. The Saviour had been laid in a borrowed manger, and now sometime later, he is in a borrowed house. Later on, he will be lifted up on a cross that had been reserved for the execution of someone else – Barabbas, an armed bandit.[3] Even in death his grave clothes and resting place were all intended for someone else.

From the outset of his life Jesus was willing to experience all these things in the place of others – of sinners.

This is the mind of Christ.

We have seen how Paul defined that in Philippians chapter 2. But here Jesus illustrates it in his life: humility

[1] James 1:22-25.
[2] Matthew 26:67-68.
[3] Matthew 27:15-23.

– borrowed stable, borrowed manger, borrowed cross, borrowed tomb. In a very profound sense, 'Foxes have holes, and birds of the air have nests, but the Son of Man has nowhere to lay his head.'[1] This is so contrary to the way 'the Palace' does things and expects things to be done. *But it is God's way.* All the more reason why we need to learn the lesson: the Lord Jesus is not found among the great ones of this world, the wise and the mighty.[2] He came in lowliness and humility; it is those who have been brought low who seek him. And they alone find him.

The sculptor Bertel Thorvaldsen sought to depict this in his marble statue of the Christ figure in the Lutheran Cathedral in Copenhagen, Denmark. The figure's arms are extended in a gesture of welcome to all. But the statue has an unusual feature. In order to look directly into its face it is necessary to kneel. It is not possible to get a clear view of it from any other position. The point is, surely, well taken. As Charles Lamb, the eighteenth-century English essayist, once noted: If William Shakespeare were to come into a room, men would stand up out of respect for his accomplishments. But if Jesus Christ were to come into the room, the only appropriate response would be to kneel.

It has always been one of the hallmarks of coming to know Christ that those who do also want to kneel before him and worship him.

---

[1] Matthew 8:20. 'Son of Man' is Jesus' own way of describing himself.

[2] 1 Corinthians 1:26-29. In this context it is worth remembering a comment made by Selina, Countess of Huntingdon on Paul's statement 'not many were of noble birth'. She was glad he had said 'not *many*' and not 'not *any*'.

This is what these wise men did. They searched for him; they found him; they bowed before him.

And then they presented their gifts to him.

Giving

John Hopkins' 'Carol of the Three Kings'[1] retells the story of the Magi's journey and imaginatively suggests reasons for their gifts:

> Born a King on Bethlehem's plain
>   Gold I bring to crown Him again,
> King forever, ceasing never,
>   Over us all to reign.
>
> Frankincense to offer have I;
>   Incense owns a Deity nigh;
> Prayer and praising, voices raising,
>   Worshipping God Most High.
>
> Myrrh is mine, its bitter perfume
>   Breathes of life in gathering gloom;
> Sorrowing, sighing, bleeding, dying,
>   Sealed in the stone cold tomb.

Perhaps not. But they were certainly gifts fit for a king. And isn't this what Christmas is really all about – giving gifts?

[1] 'We three kings of Orient are' was written by John H. Hopkins (1820–91), originally for a Christmas pageant at the General Theological Seminary in New York in 1857. The tradition that the Magi were 'kings' seems to be related to the association of their visit with the fulfilment of such Old Testament passages as Psalm 72:10-11 and Isaiah 60:1-6. We find this association as far back as the early Christian writer Tertullian (160–225) who, relating the visit of the Magi to Psalm 72:10, 15 and Zechariah 14:14, comments, 'For the East generally regarded the magi as kings.' *Against Marcion*, iii.13.

Yes. And no.

A Christmas gift from Santa Claus is invariably prefaced by the words, 'And have you been a good boy/girl this year? Then here is your present.'

The Christmas gift from God is prefaced by the words: 'God so loved the world, that he gave his only Son ...'[1] We do not – indeed we cannot – show ourselves worthy. Christ is God's 'inexpressible *gift*'.[2] Paul writes:

> For you know the grace of our Lord Jesus Christ, that though he was rich, yet for your sake he became poor, so that you by his poverty might become rich.[3]

Precisely here lies the challenge for some people, and the reason why, even when the gospel is explained to them, it becomes transformed into something quite different in their mind. All their lives they have tried to earn acceptance with God. Even the message of God's gift causes them to think in terms of what they can give in exchange for it, or at least as a contribution to it.

But while this may sound like a good bargain, it would not be good news for sinners. It is not how the gospel works; for it would mean that God's grace ceased to be what it is – *grace!*

Here is how the gospel works: God sent his Son to us, and he gave him for us and for our sins on the cross.[4] When we trust in him we receive God's free gift of salvation in

---

[1] John 3:16.
[2] 2 Corinthians 9:15.
[3] 2 Corinthians 8:9.
[4] See 2 Corinthians 5:21.

him.[1] *Then*, when we come to trust him, and the wonder of his coming dawns on us, we find that the only thing we want to do is give ourselves to him forever:

> Alas! And did my Saviour bleed,
>   And did my Sovereign die?
> Would he devote that sacred head
>   For such a worm as I?
>
> But drops of tears can ne'er repay
>   The debt of love I owe.
> Here, Lord, I give myself away;
>   'Tis all that I can do.[2]

We do not know how much the Magi came to understand. They knew Jesus was the promised King. They knew he fulfilled ancient prophecy. It is, surely, inconceivable that they did not learn even more from the lips of Joseph and Mary. Surely at least one of them would have asked, 'What is the baby's name?' and followed up by asking the scientist's fundamental questions 'why?' and 'how?' After all, there must have been a reason he was named 'Jesus' and not 'Joseph'.

When the wise men left home and family on their uncertain quest to find the new king they did not know what lay at journey's end. In common with the prophets of the Old Testament they did not know *who he was* who had been born king.[3] But they made their way home knowing that the new king was Jesus, the Saviour. In this sense

---

[1] John 3:16; Romans 8:32; 2 Corinthians 5:21; Galatians 3:13 all make this same point.

[2] From the hymn by Isaac Watts, 'Alas! and did my Saviour bleed'.

[3] 1 Peter 1:10-11.

also the story of their journey is a forerunner of the journeys made by many others who have set out on a quest they have not understood and arrived at a destination they never anticipated – and there found Jesus as Saviour and King.

Discovering destiny

A number of years ago I heard the story of one such journey. A colleague heard it from a former colleague, who in turn heard it from a minister he knew, who in turn heard it from the daughter of a man whose funeral he had conducted. And so the story went from father to daughter to a minister to a former colleague to a colleague and then to me.

The daughter's story was this. In the last few weeks of her father's life, he told her that he had recently started coming to a lunch-hour gathering held each week in our city centre church. He had 'happened in' one day, listened, and then returned. As he sat quietly and anonymously he heard about Christ. He found himself drawn to him, and came to trust him as his Saviour and Lord. Before he died he told his daughter that he felt as though he had come to the end of a long journey and at last found the destination that had eluded him for the whole of his life. He had found Jesus Christ. Indeed he knew that he had been found by him.

The stories of such journeys can easily be multiplied. Augustine was right after all: God made us for himself, and until we come home to him we never sense that we have found our destiny. It is not surprising, therefore, that a poll published a number of years ago in *USA Today* indicated that the majority of people in every age group feel they have not yet found their destiny. Until we are found by Christ and find him, we will never discover what satisfies our deepest longings.

Are you on such a journey?

Have you experienced, like the wise men, an inner compulsion that you need to make it?

Where are you now on the road?

Have you started on the journey but been diverted?

Or have you, like the wise men, and indeed like that elderly man, arrived at the destination – faith in Jesus Christ as your Saviour and Lord?

This is the true meaning of Christmas: seeking, finding, trusting, and worshipping the Lord Jesus Christ.

> Our God, heaven cannot hold Him, nor earth sustain;
> Heaven and earth shall flee away when He comes to reign.
> In the bleak midwinter a stable place sufficed
> The Lord God Almighty, Jesus Christ.
>
> What can I give Him, poor as I am?
> If I were a shepherd, I would bring a lamb.
> If I were a wise man, I would do my part.
> Yet what I can, I give Him: give my heart.[1]

Have you found Christ yet, received his forgiveness, and given him your heart?

The Gospels tell us that one man refused to go on the journey that would lead to Christ – with tragic consequences, as we shall see in the next chapter.

[1] From the hymn by Christina Georgina Rossetti (1830–94), 'In the bleak midwinter'.

10

Post-Christmas Stress Syndrome

Not everybody thinks that Christmas is the happiest time of the year. Many people experience Pre-Christmas Stress Syndrome. The causes are fairly obvious. They range from financial pressures to the burdens placed on us by other people's expectations (or our feeling that they have them and we cannot meet them).

C. S. Lewis tells us that there are really three different Christmases.

There is the gospel Christmas which, he says is important to Christians, but of no interest, apparently, to anyone else.

And then, he says, there is the popular holiday which is for merry-making, and since he himself enjoyed merry-making and had no notion of poking his nose into other people's lives, he had nothing to say about it!

But 'the third Christmas', he wrote, 'is, unfortunately, everyone's business. I mean, of course, the commercial racket.' And for the rest of this brief essay, we find Lewis, with delicious eloquence, giving his reasons for attacking the commercial racket: on the whole, it gives more pain than pleasure; we give presents that no mortal would ever want; plus it creates a sheer nuisance with the result that we cannot get on with our ordinary shopping. But perhaps the best of his reasons is this: 'Most of it', he wrote, 'is involuntary':

> The modern rule is that anyone can force you to give them a present by sending you a quite unprovoked present of his own. It is almost a blackmail. Who has not heard a wail of despair and indeed resentment, when at the last moment, just as everyone hoped that the nuisance was over for one more year, the unwanted gift from Mrs Busy, whom we hardly remember, flops unwelcome through the letterbox and back to the dreadful shops one of us has to go.[1]

All this from the man who invented the oft-quoted description of Narnia (the land he created for his famous children's books): a place where it was 'always winter but never Christmas'. Lewis certainly believed there were unsavoury influences causing his pre-Christmas stress syndrome! Alas, as he hints, the cause is usually that the true meaning of Christmas is lost in the process of the celebration.

But there is another syndrome related to Christmas: Post-Christmas Stress Syndrome. One figure in the narrative of Christ's nativity experienced it in a major way. He

---

[1] C. S. Lewis, 'What Christmas Means to Me' in *God in the Dock, Essays on Theology and Ethics*, ed. W. Hooper (Grand Rapids: Eerdmans, 1970), 305.

is the one really dark character in the story: King Herod of Jerusalem. But he was not the last to suffer from it.

Deeply troubled

The wise men had done something we all seem to do at some point in life. They wrongly assumed that if God gave them a start (in the appearance of the star they followed), they would come to a point where they could manage the rest of the journey themselves. After all, the new king was bound to be born in a palace. That was only logical.

Or was it?

The Magi had not reckoned with the fact that the new king whose kingdom had been prophesied in the Book of Daniel was also the Suffering Servant prophesied in the Book of Isaiah.[1] And so they deduced that their intended destination must be the palace in Jerusalem. That was simple logic. Their mistake proved to be fatal, although not for them or for the new king.

Perhaps there was a language or culture barrier. In any event they took at face value Herod's encouragement to return to the palace once they had found the new king. Only a disturbing dream prevented them from doing so. Otherwise they would never have known that their first visit had left the king 'troubled'.[2]

Herod was not the kind of man who could contain such personal distress. He made sure his alarm was shared by others, so that the whole of Jerusalem was troubled

---

[1] Especially in Isaiah 52:13 – 53:12.
[2] Matthew 2:3.

with him.[1] It may seem strange on the surface that a man with theologians at his beck and call should have his equilibrium upset by the appearance of a new star and the visit of some foreign intellectuals. But Herod probably believed in astrology – and in that world the appearance of a new star symbolised the death of an old king and the birth of a new one.

Given that conviction, Herod was troubled with good reason. Hearing about this star was like reading his own obituary notice. In addition, if 'the king of the Jews' had been born as these Magi claimed, it was all the more unnerving. For although Herod claimed to be a Jew he was actually from Idumaea and probably of Edomite descent.[2] Hardly Jewish blue blood! Was this child born to be what Herod himself claimed to be – the true king? A rival king? For him, therefore, the first word of the gospel message was a threat. He must either surrender or attack.

He chose the latter and sought to destroy the Christ. Nor was he the last to respond in this way. We would be naïve to celebrate the birth of Christ without remembering its larger context within the unfolding story of Genesis 3:15. John's Gospel would make that clear right from the start: when the light comes and shines in the darkness, the darkness always seeks to extinguish it.[3]

The hostility to Christ manifested by Herod simply spreads out and increases as the Gospel story progresses towards its climax.

[1] Matthew 2:3.
[2] Edomites were descended from Esau, and not through the covenant line of Jacob.
[3] John 1:4-5; cf. 3:19-21.

If the Magi had been able to return to the Herodian Dynasty Palace in Jerusalem some thirty-three years later, this time they would have found the King of the Jews there.[4] A few hours before his crucifixion Roman soldiers would mock him using the same title the wise men had used when they came looking for him: 'Hail, King of the Jews!'[5] And had they visited the site of his crucifixion they would have found this same title written by order of the Roman Governor, Pontius Pilate, on the charge sheet hung above his head on the cross.[6] And to make it clear, Pilate had it written in Latin and Greek as well as Hebrew. The title that almost cost him his life at birth in the end did cost him his life.

But why this fear of Jesus? Had Herod responded in faith as these wise men had done, or as the shepherds did, or as Mary and Joseph did, would he have been any less a king because he loved and trusted the Saviour? No. At the end of the day, the real kingdom that Herod most feared losing was the kingdom in his own heart.

It is the same for us all until Christ masters us. People love to hear the Christmas music, even to sing the familiar Christmas carols. But often hearts seem to go cold when they hear about the true meaning of Christmas: 'Christ Jesus came into the world to save sinners.'[7] The tragic response then, whether verbalised or not, is: 'Let us sing the familiar songs whose tunes we know and love; but do not talk to us about being saved from our sins! Let us enjoy

[4] Luke 23:6-12.
[5] Matthew 27:29; see Matthew 2:2.
[6] Matthew 27:37.
[7] 1 Timothy 1:15.

Christmas without Christ!' Being deeply troubled by the birth of Jesus Christ was not only part of Herod's Christmas. It is part of every Christmas. The light shines. But the clearer it shines the greater the efforts of the darkness to resist it.

Deeply deceptive

Not only was Herod deeply troubled by the birth of Christ, but his response to the Magi was deceptive and hypocritical.

There is a great paradox here. The chief priests and scribes were summoned to the palace to answer Herod's question: Where would the Christ be born?[1] Matthew leaves us with the impression that for these students of the Scriptures this was little more than an elementary catechism question:

Herod: Where is the Christ to be born?

Chief priests and scribes: Bethlehem.

Herod: How do you know?

Chief priests and scribes: Micah 5:2: 'And you, O Bethlehem, in the land of Judah, are by no means least among the rulers of Judah; for from you shall come a ruler who will shepherd my people Israel.'

Why were these theologians so lacking in curiosity, even more so in faith? At first sight it must have seemed to the Magi that Herod was the only person in the palace with any real interest in what they were saying. But we need to look a little more closely.

[1] Matthew 2:4-6.

Herod spoke in private to the wise men. He insisted that if they found the new king then *en route* home they should let him know where he was – he would like to follow their example and honour the child himself.[1] His secrecy is easily explained. Trusting virtually nobody (the sad fate of the tyrant) Herod was doubtless convinced that if his words were overheard someone in his retinue would warn the Magi that he was a master deceiver. His whole life had been characterised by intrigue, plotting, and scheming his own advance and the security of his own position. This was a man who had passed death sentences on the wives and sons he suspected of disloyalty. With every person eliminated he probably felt a deeper sense of insecurity. And now since his rival is Christ, one way or another he too must be eliminated. That was the plan.

The first Christmas exposed Herod as a hypocrite.

'Hypocrite' is an interesting word. Usually associated with religion, the root of the word lies in ancient theatre. The Greek word *hupokritēs* was used of an interpreter or actor. In antiquity, rather than 'go into make-up' actors wore masks. Here, then, was a perfect word picture to describe someone who pretended to be something he or she was not, or pretended not to be what he or she actually was.

Jesus taught in his Sermon on the Mount that those who know they are loved and accepted by the Father no longer need to wear a mask. They have no need to pretend to God because they are conscious that he knows them already and loves them. They have no need to pretend to

[1] Matthew 2:8.

others because they are secure in their relationship to their heavenly Father – what significance does the opinion of another human have in comparison?[1] But if we lack this there will always be times when we need to wear a mask – just like Herod.

So this was poor Herod's condition as he drew near to the end of his life. Here, in the face of the coming of the new king, he was haunted once more by his insecurities. Yet what harm would the infant Jesus do to him? The Father had sent him into the world to deliver us from our fears and anxieties, and indeed from the ultimate source of all insecurities – our fear of death.[2] With the gift of his Son the Heavenly Father was willing to give 'grace upon grace' to everyone who trusted him.[3] But Herod, like others in his family after him, had already gone too far. He must destroy Jesus, even if it involved the 'collateral damage' of the young boys in the Bethlehem area. His pretence and then his savagery were both masks covering a hardened heart.

There is a principle illustrated here. When presented with the message of Christ the King we must either yield or begin to find ways of defending ourselves against his perceived threat to our lives. Deceit may be the result. It comes in various guises. We pretend to be something we are not – secure when we are insecure; claiming not to believe what we know deep down to be true; pretending to be religious or even Christian when in our hearts we resist the Saviour.

[1] See Matthew 6:1-34.
[2] Hebrews 2:14-15.
[3] Romans 6:23; 8:32; John 1:16; Ephesians 1:3-14.

Herod vividly illustrates what we have seen Paul demonstrate in Romans 1:18-32. There he stresses that God has so clearly revealed himself in the created order, and in man's life as his image, that we can never escape the knowledge of him. Deceit becomes our defence – although it cannot defend us against him:

• What can be known about God is plain to us because God has made it plain.

• In our unrighteousness we suppress the truth:
We know God, but refuse to honour him as God.
We claim to be wise, but become fools.
We exchange the truth about God for a lie.
We exchange the glory of God for images.
We are without excuse for not trusting and loving him.

• The result? Our hearts become dark and our thinking becomes futile.[1]

No wonder Herod felt insecure. But we do not have to be large-scale characters in the historical record for this to be true of us. It can be just as true of a nobody as of a somebody.

Life with a mask on can never relieve us from our ultimate anxieties. Each day involves a kind of pretence, a series of coping mechanisms – employing a dozen things to divert us from facing ultimate reality. We can never escape from God's revelation of himself to us and in us: we are made as his image, surrounded by his handiwork, dependent upon him for every breath we breathe. It takes

[1] See Romans 1:18-25.

effort to shut God out of our lives: we have to suppress the truth; we spend energy in refusing to honour God; the idols we create require our worship; we exchange the truth for a lie. And since we can never be secure in our rebellion against God we need to encourage others to share in it with us, so that we can try to drown out our consciences with the notion that 'everybody is doing it'.[1]

But it is all a mask, a pretence, a deceit, hypocrisy. It is hiding from God. And one day the mask will come off.

Tragedy

In Herod's case all this finally exploded in the infant pogrom he ordered.

There is something unspeakably tragic about this. For with Christ, how could a person feel insecure, or need to pretend? In the birth of this baby born to be king lay the remedy for all the sicknesses of Herod's soul, not to mention the sins of his life. How tragic then when someone – Herod-like – attempts to preserve his or her little kingdom or empire, rather than release all of these ultimately insecure possessions, and his or her whole life, into the hands of such a gracious Saviour and King!

Herod failed in his attempt to destroy Christ. He can never be destroyed. Herod should have known that. His own magi could have told him since they knew the Scriptures so well. Indeed it is possible that the Magi from the East could have told him if they knew about the visions of the greatest of the Magi called Daniel:

[1] Romans 1:32.

I saw in the night visions,

> and behold with the clouds of heaven
>> there came one like a son of man,
> and he came to the Ancient of Days
>> and was presented before him.
> And to him was given dominion
>> and glory and a kingdom,
> that all peoples, nations, and languages
>> should serve him;
> his dominion is an everlasting dominion,
>> which shall not pass away,
> and his kingdom one
>> *that shall not be destroyed.*[1]

If only Herod had asked the Magi if they knew anything about the life and ministry of Daniel in Babylon.

If only Herod had laid down his stubborn pride before the new king whose kingdom lasts forever and cannot be destroyed.

But Herod was determined that he would not give in to the new king.

Herod's failure

Our focus here is on the dark side of Christmas. God providentially warned the Magi not to return to their land *via* Jerusalem. In his rage Herod ordered his soldiers to kill every son born in the vicinity of Bethlehem during the previous two years. Bethlehem was a small town. Perhaps not many boys were involved. But one son lost was one too many. Before this scene even the most radical modern

[1] Daniel 7:13-14.

secularist reared in post-modernity is forced to draw the line and acknowledge that, after all, there are some moral absolutes that ought never to be transgressed. Murdering children is one of them.

Evil – and a God of love?

Yet there is a troubling element to these events. The coming of the Saviour led to the death of children and the destruction of families. The fact that there are moral absolutes does not in itself silence the question: Why would God allow this to happen?

This is not the appropriate context for a full discussion of the problem of evil. But this is an event that demands a few comments.

First, we must not be deceived by false thinking here. The death of these boys took place within the context of the birth of Christ. It was not however *caused* by Christ's birth but by Herod's sin. Here again we must be clear-sighted and understand that *correlation* is not *causation*.

• The massacre of the infants took place in the context of Christ's birth – in this sense there is a correlation.

• The massacre of the infants was caused by Herod – in this sense there is no causal relation between Christ's birth and the death of the infants. Herod alone is the causation.

Second, we should notice that, when such questions are asked, there is frequently a certain double standard applied that renders the questioner suspect. For one thing such questioners frequently insist on human freedom. But if this is granted it is illegitimate to demand that there be moments in which God should be required to place that freedom in abeyance and temporarily suspend the principle that actions have consequences. We cannot demand human freedom on the one hand and then demand that God over-ride it to convenience us when we are about to sin, in order that we may be safeguarded from the principle that actions have consequences.

But this would bring no comfort to the families where Herod's sin cost the lives of their sons. Does the gospel say anything to them?

We are not God; we do not understand all his ways. His ways are as far above our understanding as the heavens are above the earth. But what we do know is that any who grieve because of the darkness of this world can find comfort in the light of God. In the new King all who sorrow and mourn and feel pain and injustice can find hope.[1] What Jesus would later say to Peter he can say to all: 'What I am doing you do not understand now, but afterward you will understand.'[2]

The Innkeeper

In his poem *The Innkeeper* John Piper wrestles with this question and rightly answers it by pointing to the cross. It is the place where God proves his love.[3]

The poem imagines Jesus returning to the place of his birth in Bethlehem some two weeks before his own crucifixion. He discovers that after Joseph and Mary had

---

[1] As he promised, for example, in Matthew 11:28-30.
[2] John 13:7.
[3] See Romans 5:8; 8:32.

left with him, the innkeeper (Jacob) and his family had suffered grievously in Herod's infant pogrom. Jacob lost his wife Rachel and his two sons Joseph and Benjamin – and an arm as he sought to protect them.

The innkeeper describes how the soldiers came:

'But in one year the slaughter squad
From Herod came. And where do you
Suppose they started? Not a clue!
We didn't have a clue what they
Had come to do. No time to pray,
No time to run, no time to get
Poor Joseph off the street and let
Him say good-bye to Ben or me
Or Rachel. Only time to see
A lifted spear smash through his spine
And chest. He stumbled to the sign
That welcomed strangers to the place,
And looked with panic at my face,
As if to ask what he had done.
Young man, you ever lost a son?'
The tears streamed down the Saviour's cheek,
He shook his head, but couldn't speak.
'Before I found the breath to scream
I heard the words, a horrid dream:
"Kill every child who's two or less.
Spare not for aught, nor make excess.
Let this one be the oldest here
And if you count your own life dear,
Let none escape." I had no sword
No weapon in my house, but Lord,
I had my hands, and I would save
The son of my right hand … So brave,

O Rachel was so brave! Her hands
Were like a thousand iron bands
Around the boy. She wouldn't let
Him go, and so her own back met
With every thrust and blow. I lost
My arm, my wife, my sons – the cost
For housing the Messiah here.
Why would he simply disappear
And never come to help?' They sat
In silence. Jacob wondered at
The stranger's tears.

                                    'I am the boy
That Herod wanted to destroy.
You gave my parents room to give
Me life, and then God let me live,
And took your wife. Ask me not why
The one should live, another die.
God's ways are high, and you will know
In time. But I have come to show
You what the Lord prepared the night
You made a place for heaven's Light.
In two weeks they will crucify
My flesh. But mark this, Jacob, I
Will rise in three days from the dead,
And place my foot upon the head
Of him who has the power of death,
And I will raise with life and breath
Your wife and Ben and Joseph too
And give them, Jacob, back to you
With everything the world can store,
And you will reign for evermore.'[1]

---

[1] I am grateful to Desiring God Ministries for permission to quote

A bigger picture

In all our thinking about the nativity of Christ we have tried to keep in mind that his coming was the climax of a lengthy conflict that was inaugurated by God's word of judgment on the serpent following the Fall:

> I will put enmity between you and the woman,
>   and between your offspring and her offspring;
> he shall bruise your head,
>   and you shall bruise his heel.[1]

Herod's cruel deed was not an isolated event. It signalled the onset of the critical stage in the centuries-long conflict. This is dramatically portrayed in the Book of Revelation:

> And a great sign appeared in heaven: a woman clothed with the sun, with the moon under her feet, and on her head a crown of twelve stars. She was pregnant and was crying out in birth pains and the agony of giving birth. And another sign appeared in heaven: behold, a great red dragon, with seven heads and ten horns, and on his heads seven diadems. His tail swept down a third of the stars of heaven and cast them to the earth. And the dragon stood before the woman who was about to give birth, so that when she bore her child he might devour it. She gave birth to a male child, one who is to rule all the nations with a rod of iron, but her child was caught up to God and to his throne, and the woman fled into the

---

this extended section. The whole poem is available at desiringgod.org in text, audio, and video form, and is also available as an illustrated book, John Piper, *The Innkeeper* (Wheaton: Crossway, 1986).

[1] Genesis 3:15.

wilderness, where she has a place prepared by God, in which she is to be nourished for 1,260 days.[1]

John's vision here is a vivid representation of the conflict of the ages reaching its climax. The serpent has now grown into a huge red dragon (later on in the same chapter John makes this identification of 'the ancient serpent'.[2]) The child to be born is the Christ; he will rule the nations.[3] At his birth he is confronted by the great red dragon whose intention is to destroy ('devour') him. But Christ is indestructible. He is protected and preserved by God ('caught up to God').

The rest of the vision describes how the dragon then seeks to destroy the woman and the rest of her offspring but fails.[4] The whole scene is a pictorial version of the nativity of Christ, the church of God, and of the fulfil-ment of his promise that the gates of Hades will never prevail against it.[5]

If Genesis 3:15 announces this conflict, and if Revelation 12:1-6 describes its central moments, then in Matthew's account of Herod's pogrom we can detect the hand of the Evil One inaugurating its critical phase. The massacre of the infants is his desperate attempt to defeat the purposes of God. At the end of the day it is satanically inspired. But it is doomed to failure. All Satan is able to accomplish – which he does ultimately at the cross – is to crush the heel

[1] Revelation 12:1-6.
[2] Revelation 12:9.
[3] The reference to Psalm 2:9 ('you shall break them [or 'rule them'] with a rod of iron') makes this clear. Cf. Revelation 2:26-27; 19:15.
[4] Revelation 12:7-17.
[5] Matthew 16:18.

CHILD IN THE MANGER

of the seed of the woman. But that heal is crushed in the act of crushing the head of the serpent.

Herod 'the Great' died shortly after this. But his dynasty continued.

Mary and Joseph had taken Jesus to Egypt for safety (we often forget how near Egypt was).[1]

After Herod's death Joseph and Mary were instructed to return home. Joseph then heard that Herod's son Archelaus was reigning over Judaea, and 'he was afraid to go there' (with good reason). He therefore took Mary and Jesus to live in Nazareth in Galilee.[2]

Years later the brother of Archelaus, Herod Antipas ('the Tetrarch'), had John the Baptist beheaded. It was this Herod who connived in Jesus' crucifixion.[3] In due season Herod the Great's grandson, Herod Agrippa I, had the apostle James executed.[4] The last time we meet this dynasty Herod Agrippa II is mocking the apostle Paul with his sneering words: 'In a short time would you persuade me to be a Christian?'[5] What a dynasty, set against the infant child of Bethlehem!

But think about this: How extensive is the kingdom of King Herod now?

And on this: How extensive is the kingdom of King Jesus now?

---

[1] Matthew 2:13-15.

[2] Matthew 2:19-23.

[3] Matthew 14:1-12; Luke 23:6-12.

[4] Acts 12:1-2. This Herod's gruesome death is described in Acts 12:20-23. Notice the contrast with verse 24.

[5] Acts 26:28.

> And our eyes at last shall see Him,
>   Through His own redeeming love …
>
> Not in that poor lowly stable,
>   With the oxen standing by,
> We shall see Him, but in heaven,
>   Set at God's right hand on high.[1]

This is the good news of the coming of Christ.

Here in this story we discover how it is possible, like Herod, to reject Christ, and to mask our rejection of him with deceit. But the day will come when Herod, and Herod-like men and women who seek to destroy Christ and his kingdom, will stand before his judgment throne. The masks will come off. One glance from the King of kings and all their false hopes will be shattered. Humble believers, in sharp contrast, will be welcomed into the final kingdom of the Lord Jesus Christ.

There may still be a long way to go. But no power can withstand the kingdom of Christ. Not even the gates of Hades can destroy his church. He reigns. Indeed:

> Jesus shall reign where'er the sun
>   Doth his successive journeys run;
> His kingdom stretch from shore to shore,
>   Till moons shall wax and wane no more.[2]

Herod knew where the King was to be found; but he never went. The wise men came on a long journey and eventually found him.

---

[1] From the hymn by Cecil Frances Alexander (1818-95) 'Once in royal David's city'.

[2] From the hymn by Isaac Watts, 'Jesus shall reign where'er the sun'.

Have you found him yet?

Do you know where to find him?

Finding Jesus

Sometimes Christmas Eve services in churches begin with the words of the shepherds:

> Let us go over to Bethlehem and see this thing that has happened, which the Lord has made known to us.[1]

Every Christmas Eve thousands of pilgrims do exactly that – they make the journey to Bethlehem.

Others try to go 'spiritually' to the manger.

Have you ever tried to do that? It is a fruitless journey, because you never quite seem to get there.

We understand what people are trying to say in this vague but spiritual-sounding invitation. But we are being invited to the wrong place. For the Saviour who was once wrapped in bands of cloth and placed in the manger is no longer in Bethlehem – just as the Lord who was later wrapped with cloths and laid in the tomb is no longer there. He is not in the manger; he lies in the tomb no more. Where then should we go?

The nineteenth-century Scottish author and hymn-writer Horatius Bonar gives us good counsel:

> We went to Bethlehem,
> But found the Babe was gone,
> The manger empty, and alone.
> 'And whither has He fled?'
> 'To Calvary', they said,
> 'To suffer in our stead.'

[1] Luke 2:15.

We went to Calvary,
But found the Sufferer gone,
The place all dark and lone.
'Whither?' we asked.
'Into the Heavens', they said,
'Up to the Throne,
For us to intercede.'

So, then, to Heaven, we'll go;
The Babe is not below.[1]

We need to go to the *living* Christ.

Have you gone to him?

If not, go to him *now*, turning your back on your old life with all its sin, and guilt, with perhaps the shame you feel – and turn from years of hiding from God – and come in faith to trust Christ as your Saviour, and yield your whole life to him as your Lord.

Then, at last, you will discover the identity of the *Child in the Manger* and experience the *true meaning of Christmas*.

———

[1] Horatius Bonar (1808–89), 'Where is he that is born king?'